SAVING BEAUTY
Love, Healing and Multiple Sclerosis

A MEMOIR
BY HARVEY KAPLAN

IPBOOKS.net
International Psychoanalytic Books

IPBOOKS.net
International Psychoanalytic Books

All rights reserved. Copyright © 2009, 2015 Harvey A. Kaplan

No part of this book may be reproduced or transmitted in any form or by any means, graphic, electronic, or mechanical, including photocopying, recording, taping, or by any information storage retrieval system, without the permission, in writing, from the publisher.

IPBooks, International Psychoanalytic Books
25–79 31st Street Astoria, NY 11102
Online at: www.IPBooks.net

ISBN: 978-0-996-5481-3-7

Printed in the United States of America

Book Design/Layout by: Maureen Cutajar

For Suzanne
Whose memory is bathed in beauty and courage.

Testimonials

In *Saving Beauty*, Harvey Kaplan has written a very beautiful and moving book. There is a nobility about his disabled wife, Suzanne, as surely as there is in Harvey, her loving and empathic caretaker. The reader feels deeply for the difficult path taken by both of their lives, and perhaps never again will take a loved one's state of health or presence for granted, or, indeed, our own. The book is engrossing reading, as we watch Suzanne's beauty and strength diminish over the years, and observe Harvey gradually becoming a deeper and more compassionate human being. Kaplan writes frankly, openly, and sincerely. As a result, he has created a moving and heart breaking book.

    Alma H. Bond, Ph.D., al ma_bond.tripod.com, author of 15 published books, including *Margaret Mahler: A Biography of the Psychoanalyst*.

These days, so many more of us confront the transient nature of life. In fact, it seems one must love transience in order to love life itself. Dr. Kaplan's book about his marriage, his wife, Suzanne, and the love they shared is moving but its analytic precision enhances its emotional power, creating a memorable and special experience for the reader.

Saving Beauty is an absolutely marvelous book. It is at times sad and at times moving and humorous. Throughout Dr. Kaplan writes of his love and marriage to Suzanne with a consistently high level of analytic precision.

    Richard Bey, radio and TV Host

Saving Beauty is a wrenching memoir of loss and a passionate love story at once. Harvey Kaplan writes directly from the heart and with uncommon insight and honesty.

    Hilma Wolitzer, author, *Doctor's Daughter* and *Summer Reading*

An exceptionally intelligent, sensitive and brave account of serious illness as it impacted a marriage. Dr. Kaplan's book is a dramatic contribution to our lives that challenges many of our cherished assumptions about health and illness, love and devotion. The ingenuities Kaplan and his wife (also an analyst) brought to the amelioration of their unrelenting dilemma, and their struggles to extend their lives together, make for an extraordinarily moving narrative.

    David Hoddeston, Ph.D.
    Professor English, Rutgers University

When my life is thru
And the angels ask me to recall
The thrill of them all
Then I shall tell them
I remember you

Johnny Mercer

Acknowledgments

I would like to thank the many people who I have met in the course of writing this book. The many who have bravely battled this difficult disease and the many who have been on the other side of the struggle – writing, researching, and working to create inroads to forging greater compassion and possibilities for cure. I would particularly like to acknowledge my friends and family who have stuck by me through thick and thin. In particular, my daughter Caroline, for her unfailing support, Enid Harlow, for her cogent observations about the structure of the book. And especially my friend and editor David Salvage, for having the vision and energy that believed in the importance of this book at its earliest stages of conception.

Contents

CHAPTER ONE	I've Got You Under My Skin	1
CHAPTER TWO	Send in the Clowns	25
CHAPTER THREE	I Believe in You	37
CHAPTER FOUR	The Party is Over	57
CHAPTER FIVE	These Foolish Things Remind Me of You	69
CHAPTER SIX	Memories of You	75
CHAPTER SEVEN	Try a Little Tenderness	99
CHAPTER EIGHT	You Make Me Feel So Young	115
CHAPTER NINE	Put Your Dreams Away	131
CHAPTER TEN	I'll Never Smile Again	145
CHAPTER ELEVEN	Moonlight Becomes You	159
CHAPTER TWELE	I'll Be Seeing You	173

SAVING BEAUTY
Love, Desire and Multiple Sclerosis

Chapter One

I've Got You Under My Skin

I sat beside my wife at Roosevelt Hospital watching her gasping for air. Her eyes widened with terror and her abdomen continued to suck in just enough oxygen to survive. The multiple sclerosis eroded the strength that her lungs needed to fight infection. The ICU consisted of a warren of cubicles and thinly drawn partitions and flashing lights. In each one a different tragedy was unfolding, heart attacks, strokes, and sudden deaths occurring at different moments when the tubes and wires that separated the living from the dead were unplugged forever.

Her eyes gleamed up at me like dark brown stones against the starched institutional sheets.

Her fingernails dug into my hand.

"I feel like a forgotten woman." She gasped, and then fell back against the pillow as a narcotized current pulled her under. Bells rang and an army of interns and nurses convulsed in a frenzy of activity behind the curtain, pounding on another patient's chest, calling out for epinephrine and oxygen. Fists cracked bones, beating the heart back into breathing. I stared into Suzanne's enormous eyes to calm myself, her hand now limp in mine, and saliva ran down the edge of her mouth.

"No," I whispered slowly, pressing my lips to her pale damp skin. "I will never let that happen."

A haze engulfed her eyes like a fog obscuring a ruined city. Incoherent words bubbled from her lips, as if rising up from the ocean floor, from a layer where light cannot penetrate. I closed my eyes wanting to shut out the circus of noise and death and the spectacle of blazing electric signals and monitors.

"No," I repeated to her, "You are eternal."

Suzanne had been hospitalized two weeks earlier, due to complications after a surgery. She had been battling multiple sclerosis for over twenty years and we were both veterans of coping with hospitals and medical promises and insurance claims. Suzanne's eyes closed and she pulsed in an uneasy rhythm, as if her body were fighting the respirator. The doctors making rounds spotted me and came over now that the commotion in the adjacent cubicle had subsided. The chief physician tried to sound casual as he took me aside into a quiet area lit by fluorescent lights. He told me that Suzanne wasn't responding to the antibiotics and her fever was raging out of control. They didn't expect that she would ever leave the hospital. There was limited use to the arsenal of machinery pumping oxygen and fluid into her body to maintain its homeostasis. As I digested this information, her physician touched my arm as if he were a priest granting me absolution. "I know this isn't easy but you're going to have to make a tough decision. What do you want to do about the life support? We think it's futile."

"I don't think she would want to be on life support."

"Well, the only way we can disconnect it is with your permission and her living will. Take your time. This may be the hardest decision you make in your life."

Suzanne and had I met at a party given by mutual friends in 1976. I'd been divorced from my first wife, Zoe, for eight years, but remained friendly with her and close to our daughter, Caroline. I'd had several love affairs since the divorce. They were passionate, yet I wasn't ready for a real commitment. I was restless for adventure but cynical that the wild intoxication of lovers transforming passion into the fabric of permanence could shape the contours of my life.

Never much of a partygoer, I forced myself to attend this one, on the off chance I'd meet a special woman who would share my dreams and travel with me to exotic places I still yearned to visit. I stood off to one side of the room feeling out of place, nervous and ill at ease sipping a gin and tonic. As I observed people talking and flirting, I envied their ability to mingle with ease, their lack of self-consciousness. In retrospect, the room was merely a blur–people meshed together, snippets of conversation occasionally rising above the murmur of people flirting, sipping wine and exchanging snatches of insight and gossip. While locked in my own thoughts and staring into space, I felt the presence of a woman next to me.

"Hello," she introduced herself. "I saw you from across the room and thought you looked interesting."

I managed a shy smile, attracted to her self-assured, forward manner. Suzanne took my arm and with an effortless animal grace, she glided both of us through the room, completely at home in her body. Soon we were sitting on a large velvet couch, nursing our drinks she talked about herself with confidence. Her father was a general practitioner, her mother an assistant social worker. I learned she had a brother named Frederick and had grown up in Pikesville, Maryland, a well-to-do suburb of Baltimore. She worked as a social worker and therapist at Riverdale Mental Health Center and had majored in English at the University of Maryland. I told her I was also a therapist, with a doctorate in psychology from Rutgers University.

I was caught between the slow relaxed buzz of our conversation and her compelling presence sitting next to me. Suzanne's thick black hair flowed like a dark syrup around exquisite pale shoulders. Her movements exuded the authority of someone who expects that life is destined to have a happy ending. By contrast, I was edgy and nervous, divorced and cynical about love, rarely comfortable within my own skin. When we ran out of small talk, the two of us drifted apart to speak with other people.

I'd planned to meet a friend after the party, but didn't want to leave without Suzanne's telephone number. I found her at the back of the room talking with a girlfriend. I waited until she saw me. When she did, she excused herself and came over.

"I'm leaving now," I told her, "but I'd like to see you again."

"Don't go."

"I promised to meet a friend."

"Don't meet your friend," she teased. "Take me out for a drink instead."

I smiled, feeling bullied, and assured her there would be a next time. Another woman being that assertive would have annoyed me and given me second thoughts. But Suzanne's confidence that the two of us would connect filled me with her natural buoyancy. I had lost the edgy ennui I had felt when I entered the party just two hours earlier.

"There's no time like the present." She sipped her gin and tonic and gazed with quiet confidence into my eyes as I called my friend, explaining that I would be delayed.

Twenty-eight years later I sat by her bedside in Roosevelt Hospital wondering whether there might be a reversal of fate. The doctors departed in a cloud of technical jargon as they completed rounds on the other patients. By now I knew how frequently the doctors were wrong, the limitations of medical knowledge, that illness is an unpredictable shifting pattern of climate. I indulged in a prayer that she would rally one last time, whether there might be a future of a few more years. I stroked her hair and traced my index finger down the pulsing of the arteries in her neck. She turned as if moving underwater. Then the sound of her breath became louder, like a saw cutting into metal. The vision of her possible recovery froze in my mind, like film caught in the sprockets of a projector, burnt by the fire of the bulb. Instead I contemplated the empty apartment, a solitary ending to the rest of my life.

A chronic degenerative illness time plays tricks on the patient and the lover. It dilates and twists, accelerating. Just one month ago, we were both filled with hope as we visited New York Hospital, prepared for what should have been a routine procedure. I could never have imagined that life could disintegrate in the flashbulb of a few days of accelerated decay. Suzanne required a device called an *ileal chimney* inserted into her abdomen. The surgery consisted of isolating a piece of her small intestine through a stoma that would protrude half an inch through the skin. A drainage bag was connected via a small tube that emerged from her stomach like an obscene plastic blemish, filling with yellow urine. This procedure was intended to allow her to lead a more normal lifestyle, liberated from the need for diapers and the shame of incontinence.

Suzanne was frightened of the operation. She'd been beaten down for years by the disease and the alterations of her body. But we'd been assured the surgery was routine, and the physician had performed it hundreds of times. "I don't know Harv, I just get a bad feeling about this. Call me superstitious. I just do."

"Just think of our condo in New Jersey," I reassured her, wanting to distract her from her fear. "Think how you'll love convalescing out there, surrounded by nature, watching the Canada Geese soar in perfect formation over the lake."

Suzanne thrived in natural surroundings. She had inherited a love of trees and plants and flowers from her parents. In 1989 we'd purchased a condo in Montague, New Jersey, near the three-mile, man-made Highpoint Club Lake, so that she could be surrounded by nature. Our Dodge minivan was equipped with a hoist that allowed her to move in and out with relative ease. Later we replaced the front seat with one could be lowered and raised – helping Suzanne get in and out with her wheelchair.

According to our plan, after leaving the hospital she'd go to New Jersey with her caregiver, Mana. They would live in the condo, and I'd take the train up to be with Suzanne on weekends. The two of us would spend weekends and summers in the country together. We planned to continue our life together so that Suzanne could be closer to nature–something she craved after being confined to our Manhattan apartment for so long.

The surgery occurred at a time when we were expanding, planning, expanding into a new plateau of her illness. We were renovating the apartment in the city, making it more comfortable for Suzanne. In the face of her disability, the angle of the stairs, the sharp edges of furniture, hinged doors, the slippery surfaces of marble bathtubs had all become sinister enemies, waiting to propel her toward her next fracture, her next bruise, her next potential fatality. I was creating a wheelchair-friendly bedroom by replacing a conventional door with a large sliding door that made it easier for her to enter and leave the room. For months, the bathroom had undergone a major re-configuration as we had the sink replaced, the tub ripped out, and a huge space with a central drain installed so her waterproof chair could be wheeled straight into the shower.

"It will be so easy for you," I assured her. "You can just sit in the chair and take a shower. You can take two or three a day, if you like."

I'd put off this renovation for months. A knot rose up in my stomach when I thought of living in an environment that reminded me of hospitals and nursing homes. Over the years we had both sacrificed so much, rearranged our lives and expectations in endless ways in order to adapt to the illness. The renovation hung over me like a cloud, promising finality: *It's come to this. Even your apartment is an institution.*

"When is it going to be done?" Suzanne kept asking, fearing this would become another of my famous unfinished projects.

Her innate intuition had begun to sense my resistance. She often understood me more than I did myself, fathomed the shifting of my moods, my oscillations between hope and despair. I wanted to bury my face in her breasts and summon up courage, the way I had in the first years of our marriage when her confidence gave me a sense of power, a reprieve from my earliest years of cynicism. But now she was denuded down to withered flesh, her breasts amputated, her body flickering like a machine that could signal intermittently and under precise conditions. But that afternoon her voice was strong and insistent against all odds.

"Harv," Suzanne often teased me. "If I have to listen to a description of another one of your projects, I'm going to scream. Did you ever hear the word *finish*? It's a common word in the English language."

Secretly enjoying her spirited reaction, swearing to complete the bathroom project. Years of illness had almost smothered Suzanne's vibrant insouciance, and I relished its rare appearances.

"When?" she asked again.

"Soon." I put my hands on her shoulders as if she were a fragile sculpture, resurrected from the ruins of an ancient city. Her eyes were warm bright lights gleaming against her creamy skin, seeing right through my evasions, rendering me an awkward boy hiding the guilty secret. Her expression told me that she understood, and approved, and yet she would still command the hauteur of a queen, sitting high on her throne, waving her scepter ever as she understood what her king refused to acknowledge: I needed to assert that I was not disabled. I was not disappearing into a wasting illness. Her illness ineluctably pulled me closer to the conditions of my passion for her, but to the conditions of my own terms of living and dying. In the end, if I lingered on would I be able to face the anguish of a nursing home, wearing diapers, helpless, at the whim of family and strangers for food and being taken to the toilet. Her illness brought the shadowy glimmer of the end of my own life into radical focus. I had always imagined death as a sudden breeze, my life extinguished in a merciful flash that would descend without warning. After a few more weeks of ambivalence, I hired a contractor and he completed the final touches on the bathroom while Suzanne was hospitalized, safely out of the way of the dust and fumes and drilling. But by then bacteria multiplied in her bloodstream. The ending we'd been staving off for years was overtaking us, sweeping away the small victory of a few more years by a lake with a garden , that we had counted on.

Looking down on Suzanne struggling with the respirator, I searched beyond her drugged lethargy for remnants of that assured woman at that long-ago party who captured my attention with the gestures of her hands, the thrill and seduction in her voice as she murmured through the idle waves of chattering voices. "There's no time like the present." I heard her voice in my ear again, soft but insistent. It wasn't simply a promise to a sensual world, but to an existence where possibilities would be realized, where dreams could take off and become realities. I called my friend and told her I wouldn't be meeting her later that night after all. Suzanne and I left the party and went to my apartment on 25th Street, off 7th Avenue. I had arranged to borrow my father's car. She loved opera, so I played Eileen Farrell's rendition of *Gianni Schicchi* for her. We talked for hours that moved with the timelessness that precedes falling in love about ourselves and what we wanted out of life. As we delved into our pasts and sketched our futures, I saw more than what we had in common but what we could create together. Listening to her languid voice as she ran her hand through her mane of dark brown hair, life sprawled before us as a great mystery that knowing each other would solve.

She had an adventurous nature, loved to travel, and made friends wherever she went. After she graduated from college her wanderlust had propelled her to live in Germany for a year, working in a department store, learning the language, making life-long attachments. She had an affair with a German lover, which shocked her Jewish family. My first wife had been a lovely woman, intellectually accomplished, sophisticated, and academic. Suzanne embodied the social and sexual revolutions of the 1960s. A challenge to authority and convention pulsed in the way she moved her hips, ordered a drink, spoke to waiters and taxi drivers as if they were already her good friends. She lived by gut instinct, challenging my 1950s standards of conformity, consistently questioning whether civilization was worth the sacrifices it demanded.

Even during that first evening together, I noted with the trained ear of a clinical psychologist that she never mentioned difficulties in her life, other than the usual problems with family. Other women made me feel the world was smaller, confined, riddled with rules. As Suzanne spoke over a glass of white wine, the world came alive with novelty. I imagined traveling with her to different countries, sharing romance in hotels overlooking the grand lagoon with children whose eyes would be a blend of her brown and my green eyes.

Did the same fantasy images of a heaven of exotic beaches and European castles wind through Suzanne's mind or did I seem like a convenient way to spend an evening or a brief affair? Did she suspect when we met that she would one day develop multiple sclerosis and need me to support and sustain her? Was that what she grasped in the nervous, divorced man who caught her attention across the crowded room?

I learned later that when Suzanne was 27, she had been diagnosed with optic neuritis, a forerunner of MS that usually goes into remission for some time before the actual symptoms of MS appear. Her father was a doctor and Suzanne was quite literate regarding medical matters. I often wondered whether she recognized some quality in me the first time she saw me that convinced her of my capacity to see her through a long, serious illness? Of course at that time she didn't consciously know that she would become ill but a thread of almost extra-sensory intelligence ran through her intellect. At times she reminded me of a cat, sensing the coming of rain or an earthquake in a deep feral region of her brain that eluded the realm of linear logic. Did she perceive me rather as an attractive man, one who was ready to settle down? Or did I need to see her as needing me to be a provider in order to complete my own romantic vision of myself as heroic?

Psychologist James Hillman suggests in *The Soul's Code* that even on first meetings, lovers sense unfathomable imagos of their uncompleted dream lying deep within the other, drawing them to each another. The force of love rises up defying convention, causing cities to burn, armies to march in the night, masterpieces to adorn the ceilings of cathedrals. What could Suzanne have seen in me that made her walk across the room to my side? "Not attributes and virtues," Hillman contends, "not voices or shapely hips or bank accounts, not projections left over from earlier flames or hand-me-down family patterns, simply the uniqueness of this person whom the heart's eye selected."

Maybe she glimpsed the role I would play in her illness without yet fully understanding that she might become ill. That night and in the first years of our marriage the idea of illness and mortality were banished like a vapor burning off through the heat and tenderness of my mouth on hers. In marrying her, my life achieved a purpose and meaning it would have lacked without her. And then she became not merely "sick" in the generic sense of the word, rather her life script changed into one where the ease of getting what you wanted changed into a story of struggling against a tide crashing against the shores of her body without mercy, eroding the core of her existence. It's impossible to know what direction my life would have acquired had I not met Suzanne. The road not taken is a complex and seductive possibility that leads into an endless forest where everything is possible but nothing is achieved. In any relationship of depth, one's partner becomes an ally and inspiration – eliciting a heroic idealism, a strength and determination one never dreamt one had. Sooner or later, most of us become disabled. The sudden deaths from a car crash, a collapsing building, a massive stroke are not as common as MS, Parkinson's Disease, Alzheimer's, Muscular Dystrophy, and a host of others that lie in wait for us as we age into the geriatric society riddled with myriad diseases. This book is not a meditation on disease per se, but on the transformative power of love that allows people to deepen their relationships in the face of illness, disability, and the ineluctable fingers of time and disease.

After the operation Suzanne recovered as expected. When I visited her in the hospital, I told her about my new plan for transporting her down the stairs of our New Jersey condo. I had resolved my ambivalence about the renovations and looked forward to resuming the rhythm of our lives. Our contractor told me he could install a ramp descending from the second level to the living room to accommodate her wheelchair.

"I hope so, Harv," she whispered. "I'm so tired of staring at the walls in our apartment I could scream. I can't wait to see the lake again. Please don't make this another unfinished project." She glistened with excitement, sitting up in her hospital bed, like a prisoner having escaped the confines of drab institutional walls, ready for new mischief.

I assured her I'd follow through, and we talked about how much she'd enjoy the country – with our amicable neighbors and friends visiting frequently. I'd come up every Friday after my last patient and stay for the weekend.

"Why don't you stop working entirely so we can live together all the time?" Suzanne asked.

"I'm figuring out a way to do that."

We were both happy that afternoon, making plans for the future. We already knew the limitations her illness imposed but together we dreamt of the garden, trees, music. We reconnoitered about a train ride taken twenty years ago across the South of France, talking ourselves to sleep as we cradled each other in our couchette against the black velvet sky, then waking into the first glinting sun on the Cote d'Azur and the breast shaped slopes of the alps softening as they reached the sea. We inhabited what Jung called the mythic world of time, where dream and reality are fused, and counting the days and years become meaningless. We would be together without the interference of work and conferences. I had invested in the stock market successfully. Soon I would retire and we would be together. I envisioned good years of gardening and vintage films and dinner parties.

Three days later, a pseudomonas infection percolated in her lungs. For the next three weeks, her doctors blitzed her with an arsenal of antibiotics with polysyllabic names I couldn't pronounce. They told us they expected her to make slow but steady progress as the infection ran its course. Suzanne was discharged from New York Hospital on Monday, October 18.

I took her home and put her to bed. She came off the stretcher like a rag doll in my arms, almost comatose. Her arms and legs hung down lifeless, useless vestigial appendages. Her brown lively glazed over in a cloud of drugs and confusion. She struggled to lift her head. Mana, her health aide, fed her specialized fluids, so she wouldn't swallow water into her lungs and suffocate.

By that time, Mana had been living with us for five years. Formerly a physician in Kiev, Mana worked as a caregiver in the United States to help provide for her elderly mother and put her daughter through law school back in Kiev. She was extremely cultured and loved opera. She and Suzanne spent hours debating the merits of Maria Callas versus Renata Tebaldi, which singer had inhabited which doomed vengeful princess with greater vocal skill and dramatic technique. I imagined Suzanne living several more years filled with music, flowers in the garden, and times when I would hold her hand and feel the devotion pulsing between us, even as she faded. I enjoyed the ride to our country home – the dense urban world giving way to the primordial landscape of trees and lake.

These fantasies ran through my mind as I sat by Suzanne's bedside in Roosevelt Hospital on Election Day, alternately reading the paper and glancing at her face. I reached over and caressed her hand, recalling the ring I'd once placed on her wedding finger. We were married in June 1980 at The Explorer's Club on 70th Street, off Madison Avenue. It was a fitting place for us to marry, for the club was founded by a group of inveterate explorers, including Admiral Byrd, who investigated the most remote areas of the world without fear. A huge, white polar bear greeted us from the top of the staircase. Suzanne floated down the aisle like a dancer, her mouth, a subtle bloom of color opening against her alabaster skin. Our theme song, "I've Got You Under My Skin" filled the air with sex and yearning. Sinatra's voice contained the essence of my contradictions and released them in song; the desire toward her and at times my frantic attempts to move away from her. At forty-seven standing at the altar, waiting for Suzanne as she floated down the aisle like a swan veiled in white, my body flooded with feelings of loss, renewal, and trepidation. And then, a certainty caught fire in each breath as we exchanged vows, committing ourselves and each other to eternity, in sickness and in health.

Our first five years as husband and wife were the stuff of romance novels, travels to distant cities, an erotic current than ran through both of us at dinner parties, when our hands touched in a movie theater. We shared a love of music, theatre, and film, an excitement for our profession, and enjoyed a wide circle of friends, most of them also in the psychoanalytic field. We splashed in the drug like blue serenity of the Mediteranean. We ambled through the cool grottoes of Capri. We experienced a love affair with the world as well as ourselves, finding new landscapes that mirrored the sensuality and harmony that flowed between us. Suzanne adored my daughter, whom she met for the first time when Caroline was eleven years old. They hit it off right from the start, and the three of us became good friends as well as family.

As the dragons of multiple sclerosis lumbered into our lives, our world was devoured by illness, leaving us battling with the ravages of flesh betrayed by disease, struggling to hold on to some vestige of hope. We had no clue about the gradual loss of mobility that would eventually result in paralysis, adult diapers, nursing assistants, and medication regimens that left us both confused and exhausted. We didn't dream that cancer would exact the sacrifice of Suzanne's exquisite breasts or how many shoulder replacements she would endure. The many falls resulting in broken ankles and wrists. The dragon entered almost imperceptibly –a numbness in the fingers, a slight blurring of vision that increased until objects were fuzzy like an impossible image on a broken television set. Over the course of years the disease accelerated in momentum, becoming a monstrous and all-controlling invader, destroying Suzanne's body and casting an ever-lengthening, ever-darkening shadow over our lives: hers, mine, and that third life – the relationship we had created with love and expectation.

As she approached the end of her existence, Suzanne couldn't walk, raise herself from a chair, or relieve herself unassisted. Tremors in her arms kept her from writing. In the middle of the day she was overwhelmed by sensations of falling into a black abyss, sinking into the swamp of her body. She couldn't read because her eyes refused to focus properly. Conversation became a struggle because she slurred her words. She was plagued by constant, overwhelming fatigue "an inertia that represents a kind of death about myself. I try desperately not to surrender to it, but feel a strong pull to live permanently in its arms. I feel I am losing my dignity with each loss of ability to care for myself."

Gazing down at her body, flaccid against the plastic oxygen mask, the doctor's words echoed in a chamber of my brain. *No longer expected to live. We're not sure of the purpose of life-support. She has not quality of life. Don't rush. This is the hardest decision you'll ever have to make.*

Two months after we married, we took possession of a co-op on Broadway and 76th Street, not far from Lincoln Center, putting us within walking distance of the ballet, concerts, theatre, and Suzanne's beloved opera. At age 39, Suzanne still hoped to have children, so we chose an apartment with three bedrooms. Sometimes after we made love I would stroke her abdomen, imagining that a filament of seed had caught and that a helix of our combined DNA was forming a child that would combine her good looks with my green eyes. We came to terms with our identity as a childless couple, with the fact that she would never conceive and the room meant to be the nursery would become her caregiver's room instead. Well into her middle years when people are reaching the apex of their productivity Suzanne was reduced down to a helpless state, clawing at the air, desperate for the attention of her caregiver, trying to find the will to make it to the next hour.

We threw ourselves into decorating the apartment, buying furniture, planning the rooms. Every purchase we made, each decorating decision we settled on, seemed to solidify our commitment to one other. Our tastes meshed for the most part, but when they didn't, it was effortless to discard a piece of furniture without rancor. The energy and fire of life that we shared made questions of paint and decorative objectives fun but secondary to a more powerful love. Suzanne encouraged me to finish my psychoanalytic training, and our lives were busier than ever. I was preparing and presenting case reports, and maintaining my own analytic practice. The nights were filled with energy and discussion of the slow unveiling of the unconscious, our patients' dreams and our efforts to decode the mystery that lurked within. The unpredictable states of rage, despair and ecstasy of the men and women who lay on my couch, as I listened and filled realms of paper with notes and ideas about the roots of their trouble, the possibility of their cure.

Suzanne's schedule was equally hectic as she conducted a psychotherapy practice while continuing to work as a therapist at the Riverdale Mental Health Center. "I coasted on my looks. Now I want something more meaningful. I wanted to do psychotherapy as soon as I finished Fordham and was thrilled to get the position at the Mental Health Center in Riverdale."

When Suzanne decided to pursue advanced training in psychoanalysis, we agreed we should study at different institutes. My brother introduced her to the New York Freudian Society – he was a former president – and Suzanne opted to train there. We spent hours discussing psychoanalytic theory and clinical practice. The field of psychotherapy seemed to hold so many answers at that time – the solution to complex mysterious, unconscious riddles, and sexual enactments played out in fascinating ways. Patients who masturbated over telephone wires, who reached orgasm while a lover sat on a bedside chair weeping. High powered lawyers who stole candy secretly from drugstores. Married women extricating themselves from abuse and oblivion.

Suzanne rarely had a bad word to say about anyone. This annoyed me at times, for psychoanalysts are known for their tendency to gossip and backbite and use the jargon to put each other down. *Infantile. Hopelessly regressed. Anal fixation.* I found these activities harmlessly amusing and wanted Suzanne to join me, but could never get her involved. Suzanne liked most people unequivocally. And gradually, thanks to Suzanne, I changed from an edgy, cynical New Yorker, looking at the darker side of people's character, to someone who contemplated life as a banquet rather than an obstacle course. Her innate conviction that anyone deserves to get the best out of life rubbed off on me, and my ambitions grew larger. I wanted to give her the world but I didn't have to. There was always a beckoning universe greeting me each morning with her dark sensuous eyes, her hand stroking my chest in the morning as we lumbered out of our dreams into the daylight and the matrix of our lives, crammed with patients and conferences, and the coming of the evening and pleasure.

Sitting beside her bed in Roosevelt Hospital, my mind wandered back to a fragment of a morning two weeks earlier to Tuesday, October 19. I'd gone to my office on West 56th Street early to get caught up on paperwork and return phone calls from the previous day. The phone was ringing as I walked in the door. Mana's voice greeted me on the other end of the receiver, urgent and dense with information, explaining that Suzanne's condition had worsened. I cancelled my patients for the day and rushed home. Suzanne lay prone on pale green sheets, almost unconscious, struggling to breathe. She was burning with fever and didn't respond when I called her name or touched her. I called an ambulance and insisted the driver take us to Roosevelt Hospital, which had a noted multiple sclerosis center led by the renowned doctor, Saud Sadiq. Suzanne went there for regular checkups and various minor emergencies that cropped up over the years.

The doctor immediately placed her in intensive care and told me her condition was grave. She was severely dehydrated with both pulmonary and urinary tract infections. He offered me a sliver of hope – saying he thought there was a slight chance that she'd respond to treatment. After he left I drew my finger down her moist forehead, leaving a slight trace in her sweat, overcome with the sensation that this tenderness was tainted with guilt, with brutality, with the futility of the past two decades of ineffectual treatments rising into a final crisis. Why had I urged her to try surgery? Why hadn't I paid more attention to her fears? I knew this kind of questioning never did anyone any good, but these questions raced through my brain with a life of their own, like rats released from a cage.

Toward afternoon, the doctor approached me and asked if Suzanne had a living will, or if she'd ever indicated she didn't want life support. The question unnerved me even though I saw it coming. For the first time since her diagnosis 19 years earlier, I faced the actuality of her death. I watched, frozen with indecision, as Suzanne was connected to a respirator.

Later that evening, I left the hospital and walked the twenty blocks north to our apartment. Drifting past the shops and trendy restaurants on Amsterdam Avenue, I recalled an episode from the summer before we were married. I'd planned a trip to Greece and was excited about taking Suzanne with me. I thought she'd be thrilled to go. The elegant white islands on the Mediterranean were my ideal backdrop for the initial heat of our romance. But she'd already made plans to spend the summer in the Hamptons with her friend Judy. I'd never once considered she might want to do something other than travel with me.

"But we're talking about Greece!" I protested. Visiting the Greek Islands was a long-time dream of mine, and now in the heat of my love, I couldn't imagine seeing those bright white cliffs without her. But Suzanne remained intractable, her arms propped on a white down pillow. In those days she still smoked and she blew a slow, confident smoke ring towards the window.

"I've been there before," she shrugged, her eyes were mysterious unreadable pools that met mine with a cool determination.

We argued for the next week, neither of us giving an inch. Ultimately I went to Greece alone, hurt, disappointed, and furious. I spent several miserable weeks wandering through scenic vistas aching for her voice, waking from dreams in strange hotels feeling incomplete and amputated without her body pressed against mine.

I returned still angry, realizing how deeply she was capable of hurting me. A pain flared in my chest at the possibility of abandonment, betrayal, the vision of Suzanne driving around the mansions of the Hamptons in a sleek car with another man. But the moment I saw her, I knew I couldn't walk away from her self-confident life force. Nonetheless, I attempted a measure of authority. "Why did you take such a risk, putting our relationship in jeopardy for a house in the Hamptons?"

She looked me straight in the eye. "Because it wasn't a risk. I knew you wouldn't break up with me. You've got me under your skin. Maybe the next time you won't take me for granted and give more serious thoughts to my needs and wishes."

On Wednesday, October 20, I took Suzanne's living will to the hospital. Over the following week she lapsed in and out of consciousness. She had a few visitors – my daughter Caroline and several close friends – but she could only interact with them sporadically. I urged them not to make her talk, not to test her endurance. With her belabored breathing, it was easier for her to listen than respond. She nodded occasionally as pieces of news from the outside world filtered in, details of the election, the coming struggle for the presidency, that meteorologists were predicting a benign winter. Since her friends knew what I wanted to hear, they all told me she looked better, colluding with my wish that the grim reality could be draped over with a fabric of expectation and optimism.

After the conversation with the doctor about detaching the life support, I called my daughter, who soothed me. "Dad, you shouldn't be alone with this." I knew Suzanne didn't want to prolong her life by artificial means. We'd discussed the issue many times – more frequently as the MS worsened. Technically, the hospital could not act on its own without my permission. Part of me wanted the institution to take this decision off my shoulders. I was raised in the post-war era that believed in science as a new form of religion and decorated buildings with images of atoms. As Suzanne struggled to breathe, her fever spiking off the charts, it seemed incomprehensible that machines and technology couldn't reverse this process, even if only for another few months. And it seemed even more unjust that the hospital would ask me to deal the final blow – admitting that technology had done all it could for her.

I went home, had a glass of Chardonnay and prepared myself for this final stage that had lurked in my consciousness for the past decades, uncertain as to what I should do. If the machines were failing, it seemed pointless to go to the trouble of disconnecting them. And yet, only two weeks ago it had seemed that the surgery had worked, had whispered the hint of a promise that we would have more years together in the country as I transferred patients to younger, eager colleagues and moved out to the lake.

On Monday, November 1, I returned to Roosevelt and remained at her bedside throughout the day and late into the night, the doctors gave me a respectful distance. A nurse with grizzled hair and the rheumy eyes of an old devoted Labrador retriever advised me to go home and sleep. "She'll live through this night too," she reassured me and shooed me off into the night.

Character is the set of traits, qualities, and patterns that define who a person is and what purpose she gives her life. It encompasses her motives and the way she acts – whether she is kind or cruel, wise or foolish, generous or stingy. I recognized the power of Suzanne's strength of character the first time we spoke at that party twenty-eight years ago. When she fell ill, her character accelerated into a higher gear. The subtle pressure of mortality made her more determined to milk the present moment for meaning, to make each day a crucial experience, every gesture count. I came to see her as a warrior, a gallant and uncompromising fighter going into battle with dragons against impossible odds every day of her life. She behaved like a warrior, asking her doctors precise, carefully formulated questions. She was gracious with them, but refused to accept vague answers or questionable information. She avoided focusing on discussions of her illness in our social circles, insisting to her friends by her example that she didn't want to be pitied, she wanted everyone to have fun. She continued putting her efforts into her practice and her professional organization, pushing to expand her social world and to extend her leonine energy to others who needed her.

When we love someone profoundly, we cherish our lover's soul. But we don't often speak of this until some disaster befalls us, bringing us closer to death. Only then do we acknowledge the soul of the stricken partner, the essence of what lies beyond their body, what lies beyond their life. We glimpse an ineffable radiance in the flash of their smile that we will hold in our minds forever. We admire their graciousness, the cracks of their humanity, the white lies they tell and a myriad of tiny human failings that become all the more endearing. We feel them ignite our blood into an ancient call of battle, the refusal to surrender to the encroachments of illness and the dreariness of a life of monotony.

Even now I wish for more time before the dragons of multiple sclerosis were loosed upon us. For just another year or two of our place in the sun.

Over time I've come to understand the soul in the way James Hillman does, consisting of the luminous shimmering qualities of goodness, courage, friendship, and loyalty. A distant reflection of the roar of the sun captured and reflected across a white lunar surface transmitting life across an infinity of years through chasms of space. Character, Hillman asserts, is "soul in action." The soul is more than an abstraction, but is elicited as a person's underlying integrity or basic decency as it plays out in the every day details of life. Our character or soul imprints everything we do. Through our actions we create our individual histories, we began painting the white expansive canvas of our lives with the creation of our destiny. In more than forty years of practice as a psychologist, I have become convinced that many contemporary forms of psychotherapy have wrongly and neglected the concept of the soul. The word often conjures up a vague uneasiness of a dewy new Age mysticism, dripping across the covers of pastel covered pamphlets in health food stores, that arouses distrust. But deep, lasting relationships – be they romantic, friendly or familial – require the openness and willingness to engage our imaginations in discovering the deepest essence of the person we love. This essence is linked to the gestures and rhythms of everyday life – the way the beloved holds their fork at breakfast, curls up on a pillow, or bounces a check. All of these minute particulars constitute the fabric of life at its most textured. Those who fail to grasp this live in a bathetic two-dimensional world, devoid of poetry and the juice that animates libido. They drift from one relationship to another, dissatisfied because they cannot make this crucial leap.

This story is about love, disability and devotion. The three are ineluctably entwined like triplets wiggling in unison on one umbilical cord. In the universal struggle with intimacy, illness, aging, and death, the soul reveals the glimmering mystery of itself, and our characters have the chance to speak and bear witness to the healing power of love.

I gave Suzanne Hillman's book, hoping it might be helpful to her. In one of the tapes in which she recounted her struggles with MS, she observed:

> There are times when I feel more spiritual about myself, as discussed in *The Soul's Code*, which Harv has given me to read. That book talks about each of us as having come into this world with a unique, personal calling. I must continually grapple to find what is unique about me. Otherwise I will end up living in a

mass of confusion and desolation. Somewhere in my disability I must find the message that tells me what I have to do to continue living with hope and inspiration. I can't leave this to Harv to define for me. In the midst of feeling like I'm sinking how will I grasp at the roots of a new kind of happiness?

The nurse and the wisdom of her wise dog's eyes proved to be accurate. Suzanne lived through another night, dextrose and saline filling her veins with the rudimentary requirements of life. But her death hung heavy in the air. Not the abstract poetic death of a blissful sleep of oblivion. Now the odor contained hints of the fetid stench of actual death that the hospital detergents couldn't mask. The room smelled of the coming of rigor mortis. The white sheet draped over the body turned into cadaver. Human beauty transformed into the stuff of science and embalming fluid. The papers waited for my signature, my stamp of approval as the next of kin that we should declare the struggle should end, that life support should be disconnected.

During visiting hours at her bedside at times I gazed out the window at the distant pinpricks of stars in the sky, struggling against the dread of the next night's solitude, searching to find an answer in the pattern of Suzanne's thick dark hair which continued to grow sleek and healthy against all odds, insisting that she was still a queen, refusing to acknowledge that she had been vanquished. I studied the map of her periwinkle blue veins spreading out on her pale blue arms as if a code lurked within it that might give me a signal of the right decision. With a trace of my hand on the hospital papers the machines could be disconnected. She would disappear forever into the dark maternal night.

Chapter Two

Send in the Clowns

On Thursday, November 4, I rode in a limousine from Riverside Funeral Parlor in New York City to Riverside Cemetery in New Jersey. The long line of limousines moved along the highway in close formation. I sat in the backseat, staring out the window, my eyes focused on the sky. I thought again of how furious I had been with Suzanne for refusing to go to Greece with me all those years before.

"Why are you going on like this?" she demanded. "I didn't consciously want to ruin your trip."

"But you did ruin it," I fumed. "You did it because you weren't sure about me. You wanted to be free out in the Hamptons, free to maybe find another man."

She thought for a minute. "There's some truth in that," she conceded. "I didn't like your attitude. Like you thought you could push me around and tell me what to do."

I couldn't leave it there. "You were willing to ruin my trip," I badgered her, "knowing how long Greece had been a dream of mine."

"Oh please," she groaned with amused exasperation. "We could have gone the following year. Don't keep going on about it, Kap! Just love me."

Harvey A. Kaplan

No one had called me Kap since childhood. The soft, seductive syllable – Kap –, hit a chord that sucked me back through tricks of time to memories of my youth, to ringolevio and stickball games, stolen subway rides into the heart of Time Square, the endless wandering through the expanse of adolescence.

As the car pulled us through the damp sepulchral day towards the cemetery, my mind was like a projector, with segments of film activating at random. I would see a last leaf on a skeletal tree and remember the death of my mother. The steering wheel of the car reminded me of my father, his startling blue eyes and cigars, his firm hand on mine as he showed me how to navigate our Chevrolet through the cobble stoned streets of the West Bronx. The gray monotonous highway reminded me of a spread sheet I'd included in my dissertation. I recalled my first meeting with Suzanne's family. Suzanne introduced us soon after we'd started seeing one another exclusively. She lived with her parents and brother, Frederick, just outside of Baltimore. Her mother, Eleanor, was an assistant social worker. Frederick was interested in horticulture and later opened a hot house, which never managed to make any money. This may have been a factor in Frederick's growing resentment toward most people he knew, including me. Suzanne couldn't have been more different from her brother. Frederick was devoid of humor, his slanted dark eyes reminded me of one of the tortured saints in an El Greco painting. In contrast to Suzanne's innate confidence that the world was ripe with adventure, Frederick engaged in conversation reluctantly, with a chronic uneasiness, as if he feared a tape recorder was taking down his every word.

Their father Kennard, was a highly regarded internist, who ran their home in a dictatorial manner. The entire family, including Suzanne, feared him. Eleanor constantly smoothed over the tensions he caused. Her passivity and her habit of harping on Suzanne's social life irritated Suzanne although she concealed it effortlessly, just the slightest tensing of her spine when her mother discussed the problems of a society with no morals, the looseness of modern women, the disgusting spectacles of burning brassieres. A veneer of southern manners hung like an claustral mantle over the Yaffe household. During the years of Suzanne's childhood spent learning manners in the elaborate drawing room, studying in the library with oppressive mahogany furniture, she pretended to cooperate with the rituals of conformity while dreaming of traveling far across the ocean and disappearing into a radical new life. In the mean time she smiled and bided her time, enduring the rituals of Eleanor ringing a bell, summoning the cook when Kennard dictated it was time to bring in another course or to clear the table. Suzanne had been able to throw off the shackles of her childhood whereas I still lived with the uneasy sensation that my parents were eating me alive.

Suzanne's parents often spoke of how much they wanted grandchildren, darling dark haired children who would populate their house and bring back life into the museum like rooms on the holidays. Sweet child bodies in swimsuits glistening from the pool, cartwheeling across the glossy green summer lawn. Early in our marriage we tried to conceive, but Suzanne was plagued with fertility problems, and we ultimately gave up on the idea of children. She turned her maternal devotion to Caroline, and to fussing over me. Her infertility may have been related to her MS, but we never knew that for certain. For the first five years of our marriage, we lived in an idealized world where death and sickness were banished like ghosts, like far away stains in the rugs in dreary third rate pensions that are easily forgotten in the pleasure of contemplating the ruins of ancient cathedrals. Her episode of optic neuritis had receded like an image recorded on a palimpsest. Later, after her diagnosis, issues like her infertility haunted us like clues from a mystery that had tricked us, possessing a sinister significance now that we knew a dangerous intruder was tearing down our carefully created world. In time we came to see the infertility as a blessing, a reprieve from the possibility of a child growing into the complexities of adulthood, with the shadow of a desperately ill mother, or a dangerous gene programming it for the identical future of a debilitating illness, dragging her down across the river of time.

Suzanne's love for my daughter, Caroline, couldn't have been deeper had she been her own child. In the back of that limousine riding through the gray highways of New Jersey, I squeezed Caroline's hand and thought how grateful I was that she and Suzanne had been so close. The two of them first met when Caroline was eleven years old. Almost immediately, Caroline came to think of Suzanne as a second mother, and Suzanne once told me that if she had had a daughter, she would have wanted her to turn out just like Caroline–creative, friendly and smart.

In typical mother-daughter fashion, Suzanne and Caroline enjoyed ganging up on me. Once they even united against me in choosing a name for our cat. Suzanne and I had had a Maltese named Asta, whom we both loved but had to give away when his hyperactivity became too much for Suzanne to handle. We then adopted a female cat, and I wanted to name it Asta.

"No," they insisted in unison. They rolled their eyes in solidarity. Their conspiratorial expressions said: "Aren't men ridiculous?"

"Asta was the dog's name," Suzanne considered, resting her head in the cave of her hands. "A cat is like a woman, innately female. A cat is a creature of subtlety. She needs to have a name that will do her justice."

My second choice was Gatsby.

"No," they asserted, enjoying their new found bond. "That's a male's name." After conferring in a female enclave from which I was excluded, they arrived at another idea.

"If you like *The Great Gatsby* so much," Caroline suggested, "Why not name the cat Daisy?"

"Wonderful," I replied, "But you know, Daisy wasn't such an admirable character, but what do I know?"

"Oh Dad," Caroline sighed with exasperation, "It's a pretty name." She and Suzanne smiled at each other conspiratorially.

Daisy and Suzanne became inseparable. As Suzanne grew less mobile the cat spent hours buried into her lap as if Suzanne's body were a delicious pillow, a sanctuary for which she would fight to the death. I loved Daisy in my own way, feeding her chicken livers and pounce treats, but it was too painful for me to watch her pulling her old arthritic bones into Suzanne's favorite chair after she died. Daisy would sit on the cushion looking confused and bereft, as if trying to understand why she had been expelled from paradise. Ultimately, I placed her with friends so that she could begin a new life.

I imagine Daisy in her new home, petted, adored, the queen of the household. I imagine Suzanne too, a monarch in a new realm that mortals can't fathom, far off in the inky blackness of death, deep in the web of differential integrals that astronomers use to calculate the motion of celestial bodies. I imagine her decades ago, before we had met, dancing at her high school prom, cavorting effortlessly on her tall graceful legs, her eyes wide with excitement and expectation that the future would bring her freedom. Suzanne exists somewhere, her soul glows in a primordial darkness, far away from me in a place I cannot reach or touch.

And I sit in the apartment after the last patient of the day has left and read the papers and order in chicken and broccoli from the corner Chinese restaurant. I wonder about my own soul and what remains ahead for me as my soul hurtles through the final years on this earth.

The chronicle of life is a tapestry of complex relationships, threads of memories, bonds of love. In crisis, the bonds rise towards the surface. If the tension is too much, they may break. Friends become estranged. A lifelong enmity emerges from a thoughtless remark. A love affair blossoms against all odds for reasons no one can understand. A neurotic symptom unravels, a burst of freedom moves through the veins of the sufferer as the death instinct falls away. I consider patients histories, the stories of people I know socially, numerous memoirs chronicling the lives of the famous and the dramas they contain; bitter fights over wills, acrimonious legal battles, regrets over the things that they never found the courage to say, or the harsh remarks they would take back if they could. Unexpected passions emerging without warning, delighting lovers like the surprise gift of a violet orchid blooming against all odds in a snow bank.

If illness represents tragedy disguised as a gift, the textbooks and the media acolytes all advise us to acknowledge the gift but be open and ready to do the work, to grasp as completely as we can to the richness within the melancholy. This is how we ripen, learning that illness is not by definition a tragedy, unless we succumb to despair. We can grasp the necessity of loss and find the courage to continue living with a greater zest, more sprezzatura. We all drown now and then in the every day bump and grind of life; taxation, mortgage payments, the tedious things adult life requires us to do in order to move from one year to the next. But beneath that realm of pragmatic detail and responsibility lurks a deep primordial world that passion and illness never lets us forget. After Suzanne's diagnosis was final, small details mattered less. I didn't get angry at the dry cleaner.

I didn't care that the coop maintenance was going higher. I wasn't indifferent or numb. I felt liberated, freed from trivia, alert to the fact that I was walking through a vast canvas in which these incidents were trivial, tiny insects scurrying across the greater tapestry of love and survival. That is part of the priceless gift of illness – the rapture, the intensity of that deeper level of experience. In the shadow of the ageless themes of sex and death the clutter of modern life fades into the distance.

A few months before we were married, Suzanne decided to start her own practice. "I discussed this with Harv," she remarked in one of her tape recordings. She made these cassette recordings to remind us both not to procrastinate. She knew that we didn't have forever and was constantly urging us both to suck the marrow out of life. "I thought going into private practice full time was a bit risky because you can never be sure about filling your open hours, but Harv was encouraging. He promised he would help me to get patients, and I sighed with relief at that. I was so full of myself and my future then. It was one of the best times of my life."

Suzanne's determination to take a risk in the service of going after what she wanted illustrates the blessing of recognizing our mortality. Illness challenges us to live in the present – to avoid putting off for another day what can be done now, what must be seized and made the most of. Many forms of therapy invite the patient to ask the question: What would you be doing if fear were not an option? How do you want the words on your tombstone to define what you contributed to this life? These techniques motivate patients to break through blocks, to fathom the lives they were meant to live. Suzanne's illness brought the question of her destiny into focus like a laser. What indeed could you be doing that you aren't? If you died tomorrow, what would be unfinished? What would you have to do to feel fulfilled? How does this motivate you? How does it bring you a step closer to your destiny, your purpose on this earth, the thing that you were born to do? Deep within the engine of middle age and multiple sclerosis these questions emerged and galvanized Suzanne to go into private practice. Within a few months after her resignation her hours were filled and she worked long into the evenings with fervor, understanding other people's lives through her exploration of her own, diving deeper within herself in order to find answers to the riddles which confronted her in her consulting room.

One humid June day we marshaled our energy and braved the crowds of Broadway, shopping for furniture for her office. We bought two leather chairs, a killim rug imported from Ephesus, the requisite analyst's couch, maple bookshelves and two oval glass tables with wrought iron legs painted black. She had always dreamed of outfitting her office as she pleased. "By the way, I haven't forgotten you." She stroked me under the chin, as if I were a cat she were coaxing into a deep sensual thrill of purring ecstasy. Without ceremony she reached into her bag and extracted a gift certificate she had purchased. It was for a chair – not just any chair, but an Eames, complete with ottoman. If you were an analyst, that chair – elegant beyond the realm of any expense – informed the world that you had reached a pinnacle of success and approval. Suzanne knew that my childhood in the Bronx, my belief in saving money, the part of me that didn't have her natural extravagance that would work out the expenses and make it work out later. I wasn't yet liberated enough from my own insecurities to buy myself that chair, as much as I wanted one.

I was dumbfounded. "How could you have known that I've always fantasized about having this chair?"

"Didn't you tell me that your former supervisor had one – a man you revered? And don't I know that your brother has one?"

Saving Beauty

"Yes," I replied. "But how did you know that to me this chair represents success?"

"Because you're not as hard to figure out as you think. You idealize people and become impressed with what they have."

"Are you saying I'm envious?"

She shook her head. "I didn't say envious, I said impressed. But you won't give yourself the best. And you deserve it. And I think you know exactly what I mean."

By then we had developed marital telepathy, we often finished each other's sentences smoothly, as part of a continuum of two continuous souls, other halves that had swam into each other and united. But foolishly I wished I could be less transparent, could cultivate a cool controlled exterior that would shield me from the vulnerabilities of the outside world. The subtle pressure of Suzanne's hand traced the hairs of my hand gently, and the need to be invulnerable dissolved. Her minted mouth landed against my mouth, moist and inviting, kissing the outside world away.

The first time I sat in the Eames its rounded back gripped my shoulders, a sexuality linked with power and approval surged in my body. I was now one of the big boys, the men who made the rules, the men people came to and sought their advice and expertise. Suzanne knew this chair would have that effect on me. When she came to my office later that day and saw me sitting in it with my feet up on the ottoman, her manner was casual but insouciant as I pulled her down into my lap. We were spinning in the chair, smashing the rules of civilization and its discontents with the power of primal sex, our bodies pounding against the leather of the chair. Outside the window the skyscape filled with phallic buildings, erections of steel rising up and surging against the cloudless Prussian blue sky.

"It's true what they say," she announced, running her fingers through my thinning hair. "There's nothing like the Eames chair."

"You're the best. The very best."

She brought her face next to mine it was wet with tears.

We both knew we didn't have forever, but we did have a poignant bliss that aches with a fierce pleasure that almost hurts my body even now, thirty years later.

In September 1978, Suzanne started seeing clients at The Apthorp, one of the most majestic edifices in New York. She continued her studies at the Freudian Society and graduated in 1985. "It's been a long haul," she confided to the tape recorder. She knew what was coming – the loss of cognition, the struggle to retrieve words – and she wanted to leave a legacy.

> I feel as if I've accomplished something. The program was exciting. I worked with patients – helping them disentangle the dilemmas of their lives, listening to the most curious, perverse, dark and inspirational material that emerges from the couch, and trying to find the humanity in it all. I made a final case presentation before a committee of five analysts. They listened closely, discussed the case with me, both in the group and in private. I passed with flying colors. This event was a milestone in my professional development, but more important was the notion of healing. No life is simple. The depth and the truth of psychology comes from embracing the complexity of our species. None of us is alike. While I was at the Society, I made a host of new friends and served on committees as well as going to lectures, and continuing my studies in peer groups. And of course I had Harv. My life was full at that point.

As I continued my vigil at the hospital I thought of Suzanne's words, as I gazed at her pale misshapen body, struggling like a trapped fish gasping on the floor of a skiff. I held her words up in my mind, trying to blot out the fluorescent hospital lights. It was hard to imagine this existence attached to the oxygen mask, far away from the ability to perceive tenderness or concern, could be defined as life except as in the broadest sense of oxygen allowing chemical reactions to ignite cycles of oxidation in the sagging bag of fluid and bone that comprised Suzanne's frail, brutally fatal body. It never was clear why she became infected after the ileal chimney was inserted. The hospital declined to make any determination, however, it was obvious that there was a large gaping hole that should have cleared up were it not for the infection. In an article in the AARP newsletter it states: "Two million patients are infected in hospital each year. More than 90,000 die." I imagined the conversation we might have had if she was conscious, the words bubbling from her lips with passion. Suzanne discussing with her characteristic lack of self pity the tough lessons about endurance and determined optimism that her life had taught her, the need to stop believing in a sanitized world in which disease can be eradicated, in which the body is defined within the rigid binarism of the healthy or be damned, how we can become courageous by embracing what seems monstrous and holding it in our arms.

Chapter Three

I Believe in You

The long line of cars entered the cemetery and came to a halt. The lead driver got out and went into an office to register. I remembered sitting in another office years ago with Suzanne, filled with anxiety, awaiting her diagnosis. It was 1985, five years into our marriage. Suzanne was forty-four and concerned about a growing numbness in her fingers and feet and difficulty focusing her eyes.

We sat fidgeting in a Park Avenue waiting room covered with velvet green wall paper with small Egyptian figurines placed in glass vitrines. Our silence masked our discomfort. After a few minutes, the doctor opened his door and invited us inside. The results of Suzanne's MRI were on his desk. The doctor ran his fingers over the black plastic image of her brain dotted with patches of gray, pointing to the gray regions as if they were distant countries exploding in political revolutions that couldn't be controlled. The doctor recalled that Suzanne's bout with optic neuritis when she was twenty-seven. He attempted to sound neutral, but a tone of judgment crept into his voice, as if the neuritis were a youthful transgression that had come back to haunt her.

"What probably happened next," he surmised. "Is that it went into remission, and you were never troubled by it until now." The doctor looked down again at the MRI and shook his head, like a tired soldier admitting defeat. He believed that Suzanne had the beginnings of multiple sclerosis.

At first I refused to understand his words; artificial, clinical language extracted from a dusty textbook. What did these meaningless scientific words have to do with the woman I loved? Being diagnosed with a serious condition is like being in a surrealist movie – with two films playing simultaneously on separate screens. On one screen, adrenaline courses through your body, flooding you with terror and uncertainty, tearing the fabric of your life to shreds. On the other screen, a medical professional, often with tremendous solicitude, presents graphs of double blind clinical trials and five-year survival rates – estimating your distance from paralysis and death.

As the doctor spoke, Suzanne shrank back into the leather recliner, seeking safety in the padded cushions. A cloud moved across her face twisting her features into a mask of heated rage and confusion. Then her spine drooped and her head fell into her hands. She reminded me of a racehorse I had once seen who had fallen at the edge of the track, too stunned to comprehend the fact that its legs were useless. She gathered her second wind and started asking questions about her prognosis. The doctor winced and politely offered stock explanations about the impossibility of predicting the course of the disease, the nature of individual variation.

"Medicine isn't a crystal ball. It can't predict the future. I think it best that you get a second opinion." He beamed with generosity and gave us the name of another neurologist. I recalled having heard many years earlier that multiple sclerosis eventually leads to death. But this was an uncertain recollection and I pushed the thought out of my mind as the doctor managed a smile and reassured us, ushering us off into the afternoon with platitudes about keeping a good attitude. Later that day we walked hand-in-hand through Central Park. It was springtime, and the trees were jeweled with new buds, pushing up in a riot of life. That evening we lay on our bed, stroking each other, listening to Chopin and watching the setting sun blazing like copper across the Hudson.

Over the next few days Suzanne dissolved in tears every few hours, and numbness spread through my chest except when I put my arm around her and tried to comfort her, nuzzling my lips against the graceful arc of her neck. "We'll work this out, no matter what," I whispered and her hands gripped mine with a desperate tenacity. We didn't know the nature of the disease and had just been confronted with a confusing barrage of facts, advice, and evasions. We avoided thinking about the long-term consequences. A few weeks later the terror faded and we prepared to do battle. We marshaled our resources, gathering masses of reference books and set about learning as much as we could about this terrible illness.

"Why would our own cells attack other cells in our body?" I asked. "What perverse course of evolution could account for this? And why haven't they found a cure? They found a one for infantile paralysis, for diphtheria, for measles." Today, twenty years later, science has advanced in its understanding and treatment of MS, but there is no cure.

Suzanne was referred to an esteemed neurologist at the Einstein College of Medicine. He explained the unpredictable course of the disease, but as we left his office, he told her, "You will always be able to walk." Suzanne was pleased to hear this, but I knew by then that he had no way of knowing whether there was any truth to his assertion, and he was protecting himself from his impotence as well as us. Perhaps he needed to be optimistic to maintain a sense of hope. Clinicians, like patients, often feel helpless in the face of incurable diseases like MS. The gray institutional waiting room was filled with twitching, drooling patients, confined to wheelchairs. I wondered how he found the energy to get through that gray November afternoon.

Harvey A. Kaplan

After three months of examinations by doctors, tests, and gathering data, Suzanne prepared herself to tell her parents. We visited them at their home in the sycamore studded suburbs of Baltimore one Sunday morning. We sat in the formal dining room eating a lunch of crabmeat salad beneath the chandelier. Kennard was taciturn, and Eleanor broke the silence with her stories of society, morals were declining, the modern world was degenerating. She remembered the cotillons when girls were allowed to remain innocent until a world of brocade opened a magical path leading them into cotillions and brilliant marriages and homes with expensive chandeliers. The cycle would complete itself. When Suzanne was ready to tell them, she signaled me with her eyes and I went off into a corner of the room and read the New York Times. From where I sat, I could see Suzanne crying and at times gesturing with her hands. I imagined her as a small child, crying in the presence of the adults and hoping they would turn this terrible news into a fairy tale. Her parents remained composed, listening and gathering information.

Later Suzanne told me that her father had insisted that no one, at that point, could say with complete confidence that MS was the correct diagnosis. We wanted to believe him, but we had done enough reading and seen enough doctors to be certain that she did have MS and that her father was in denial. In the car driving back to the city Suzanne shared with me that her parents were concerned that I might leave her, and they planned to change their wills to ensure that she would be provided for. "I don't want to hurt you, it's just that they're concerned. They like you as much as they would like anyone I would marry. It's just that this is making them freak out." Illness had transformed her into their little girl again, afflicted with a mysterious illness and living a different life in a wicked city filled with decrepitude and sexual theories. In their eyes she was helpless and in need of protection. When a grave illness appears not everyone has the capacity to follow the twists and turns of the road. I've heard stories of partners disappearing without leaving a note, patients in nursing homes with tubes in their mouths and enormous lonely eyes searching the room, still unable to believe that the last chapter of their existence has left them alone with only the officious nurses marking the time and the medication records to record their passing into the next world.

The cars proceeded toward the gravesite. It was ironic that I had bought Suzanne a condo in New Jersey, where she could live, comforted and nourished by the rhythm of nature, and that now I was bringing her to New Jersey, not to live but to rest forever in the frozen earth. The endless cycle of birth and death, one dies so that another may live. Death sealed her in the ripe dark brown earth, enclosing her remains forever. I thought back to one Saturday afternoon in 1997 when Suzanne and I went for a walk in Riverside Park. We had strolled over to the animal run, watching the dogs racing up and down. By then she struggled with a cane, teetering precariously, sometimes clinging to my shirt.

"I grew up surrounded by flowers and trees," she observed, gazing at the dogs running circles across the new spring grass, gleaming with animal contentment. Then her voice became decisive, her words delivered with a slow authority like a chess move that she had been contemplating for some time. "I don't want to spend whatever time I have left on this earth surrounded by pavement. It's not the same for you. You grew up in the city and don't care about nature all that much."

"What are you asking?"

"I want a house where I can see trees. Water. Someplace near an ocean or a lake. Not just near it, Harv, but on it, with water visible from the windows." She waved her tired arm in a semi-circle, indicating the expanse of afternoon waiting to be filled, and the coming of her sickness, the days we both envisioned of her lying immobile.

"Are you crazy?" I demanded. "Do you have any idea what that would cost?"

Suzanne smiled and her eyes lit up with mischief and expectation. "If I know you, Harv, you'll find a way to do it for me."

Several years into her battle with MS we were in the middle of what Arthur Frank, in *The Wounded Storyteller* describes as the "Quest Narrative." The patient faces illness head-on in hopes of gaining something from it and becomes willing to make radical changes, questing for a greater meaning to life, giving up conventions and beliefs that are no longer essential in the service of questing for a deeper truth.

Frank views people suffering from illness as storytellers who respond to their suffering through several different narrative possibilities. The first he calls the "Restitution Narrative." In this story, the person feels that yesterday he was healthy, today he is sick, and tomorrow he will be healthy again. A patient whose cancer goes into remission is an example of this reflexive movement. The disruption of illness recedes and life restored to the terms and conditions that had previously existed. The second variation of story is more convoluted – the "Chaos Narrative": The diagnosis dictates that the sufferer will never get better, but will twist and turn on the rack of the symptoms, tortured like one of the damned souls in purgatory; waiting for the release of the spirit from the appendage of the disease-ridden tormented body spiraling out of control. The "Quest Narrative" posits illness as the beginning of a journey through which new possibilities and understandings may be gained. The patient/storyteller develops a different voice that more aptly describes the new experience of raw pain that has been given meaning. Suzanne wasn't an unfortunate sufferer, but a warrior with breastplates of armor, dictating words into a microphone:

The notions of John Donne writing centuries ago about the alchemical resurrection of the degraded body which makes resurrection possible. It's so Christian and yet it seems almost Buddhist too, to get to a world beyond the body. But what if there simply is nothing beyond the body, beyond this world. What if there exists after this movement across the earth, this movement through love and confusion if there isn't more confusion, but if there's simply nothing. I think of the winter, the animals lying in the earth. The animals in the jaws of the predator's mouth. The world as the panorama of the devourer and the devoured. Science reports that plants throb with pulses of electricity when spoken to with kind words.

That birds pine away to their deaths when they lose their mate, as if their creatures out of Plato, once having found that mythical perfect mirroring other half, they simply now that going on is futile.

That elephants emit a high moaning sound in the night, inaudible to the human ear, which allows them to communicate over hundreds of miles.

There is so much we know.

There is so much we don't know.

The milky way is a mystery at night, flecks of light like fireworks without sound.

Somewhere there must be other worlds, with people perhaps like us, or better, less prone to territoriality and warfare.

There is so much I would like to know before I go.

And so we began our quest to find a country home that would provide sanctuary for Suzanne in the later phases of her illness. I rented a car one weekend so we could start scouting the possibilities. This became our weekly excursion for well over a year without finding anything that worked. Eventually we spent a weekend with our friends Audrey and Stanley who owned a condo in New Jersey on a lake. I knew Suzanne wanted a house, not a condo, but I thought that when she saw Audrey and Stanley's place, met the other four families in the building complex, and enjoyed the splendid view of the water, she might change her mind. Soon we learned that the two-story condo next to Audrey and Stanley's was available.

The condo was a huge, two-level space with clean modern lines and magnificent light that caught the reflection of the lake. I was relieved to know there would always be people nearby if Suzanne needed help. Suzanne still had reservations, since she had dreamed of a private house. We walked into the living room, and Suzanne sat down in a chair facing the window.

"Honey, this is going to be a big adjustment. I want you to think it over and let me know if this feels right to you," I said, drawing my hands through her sleek hair, dissolving the uncertain silence that hung heavy between us. Discontent draped itself across her pensive brow. Suzanne swiveled the chair as if contemplating the verge of a precipice, wanting to back away from it at the last moment. I made her a cup of tea.

"Just think about it. That's all I'm asking. I'm going to give you some time."

She nodded.

I hiked around the lake, a two-mile walk through the autumn light glinting on the trees and the soft light reflecting from the cobalt blue water.

When I returned, Suzanne had arrived at a decision. "I think I'm going to love this view. You have no idea how happy this makes me." She sighed and her arms encircled my neck, pulling me down into the tangle of her arms.

We concluded the myriad tasks of arranging for a mortgage, conducting a title search, and ordering an appraisal to satisfy the bank that the property was in compliance with all ordinances.

We finally signed the purchase papers on a cold gray Friday in January. The lawyer gave us the key and asked what we planned to do now. I announced that we would drive back to the city.

"You're not going to spend the weekend in your new home?" he asked with a puzzled look. The deal had included furniture, dishes, towels, and even pictures on the walls. The previous owner was an elegant widow draped in a mink coat whose age I couldn't guess, who sat stiffly as she signed the documents with a spidery cursive script. She had deliberately left all of the contents of the house behind in the contract by design. Her husband had hemorrhaged to death after a radiation treatment for inoperable lung cancer in that bedroom and she couldn't bear to be reminded of their life together.

"I thought we were going to stay over." Suzanne's voice was petulant.

"Why would we do that?"

She stared at me, confusion turning to irritation. "Because it's a big day for us, and we're not going to deny ourselves the pleasure of this weekend in our new condo."

I froze. The truth is I wanted to stay in the city, safe in Manhattan surrounded by towering glass buildings and liveried doormen and twenty-four hour delicatessens. The pleasant condo frightened me – a place of dark brown colors and Eastlake furniture that belonged to someone who had bled to death; an environment surrounded by green trees and water that was linked to tragic events. As a native New Yorker, I thrived on the vibrant buzz of the city and wasn't ready to take this major step into the alien world of forests and lakes. A chasm was opening: Suzanne's disease meant giving up my comfort zone. It required me to expand in ways I never thought I'd have to. I took a breath, inhaling change in every cell of my body, and then surrendered.

Suzanne's face blazed with triumph and determination when she walked through that door for the first time as an owner. "I'm going to love it here," she exclaimed. "It has everything – space, a view of a gorgeous lake, an outside patio, an enormous bedroom." In no time at all, she had the carpet ripped up, the floors refinished, the walls painted, one wall broken down to enlarge the living room, and larger windows installed to open onto the lake. She made the place her own. Everyone complimented her taste and decorating skills.

Memories of her earliest years returned, the long ago world of her childhood, when death and disease existed only in myths and the kitchens of fairytale witches and gloomy castles where blonde girls spun their hair into ladders of gold and saved their lives. The simple pleasures of gardening and watching the seasons change gave her the feeling that she and her illness were one with the cycle of nature. The symphony of the first great storms, the earth covered over in white like death, everything glinting in brilliant pure light. Then the ground turned muddy, the occasional rank smell of dead animals wafting up from the newly warming earth, the swollen streams gushing forth with release as the sun grew high and powerful; the light blue of the lake in springtime and then the obscene blush of summer. Bone meal for the roses. High potassium fertilizers for the electric purple bloom of the azaleas and rhododendrons. Bulbs planted into the earth in the fall as the trees turned skeletal again, a promise of a new life down in the brown dirt that would resurrect in small controlled explosions of color when the sun burned the earth again. Birth, love and death made sense against a backdrop of dogwoods and owls hooting in the dusk. We made friends in New Jersey and spent almost every weekend there, leaving the city Friday afternoon and returning late on Sunday. This helped Suzanne endure the days of confinement in our city apartment, nine stories up in the air of the upper west side, sandwiched between tall glittering buildings the color of bones. "When I get to Montague and watch the sun rise and set on the lake," she observed, "I feel that my life is beginning again."

In later years when Suzanne could no longer walk, she thanked me for insisting on a condo. A private house would have isolated her.

Saving Beauty

When we reached the gravesite, I got out of the car and stood by the casket in the November chill. A rabbi recited a prayer in Hebrew that I didn't understand, but assumed to be about Suzanne's soul going to heaven. Then the coffin was lowered into the grave. I was the first to take the shovel, dig into the earth, and scatter soil on the coffin. The sound of soft earth hitting hard mahogany echoed as the first clod of soil obliterated a patch of late afternoon sun glinting on the shiny wood. After me, the other mourners took turns with the shovel. When we had all finished, I looked down at the coffin and thought how snugly it fit into the ground.

Two hours earlier in the funeral parlor, I had been asked to make a last positive identification of Suzanne before the coffin was sealed. Her features had been carefully arranged into an expression of serenity. The twisting bloom of her puckering mouth against the hospital sheets was smoothed down into a placid smile of acceptance. Her dark brown curls spilled out around her shoulders, resurrecting her pre-Raphaelite beauty for the last time. There were no vestiges of the crippling disease that had been attacking her body with such vengeance for so long. My chest constricted like a box fighting back tears, wondering how many years it would take until I would join her. I couldn't bear the slow lingering death she had endured. I wanted a stroke, a heart attack, something sudden and total that would come upon me in my sleep, would take me out like a white bolt of lightning moving from heaven through the earth.

They gave us the largest room in the funeral home, but the crowd still overflowed to the edges of the door. Suzanne's friends paid tributes to her. When it was my turn to speak I tried to keep my emotions under control, but I couldn't. I would speak and then sobbing burst from my chest like a caged animal, insisting on running unimpeded through the forests of night. Years of love and struggle unscrolled before me like a film, images of Suzanne bleeding into each other as I talked about how she had introduced herself to me at that party years ago. At the conclusion, I faced the coffin and said, "I will never forget you, Suzanne, or our life together. I will always have you under my skin."

"Was it destiny?" I asked myself on the drive back to the city. "Was Suzanne the reason I was put on this earth?" Certainly, fate had had a hand in bringing us together at that party and presenting me with the biggest challenge I had ever known–a challenge I was not even consciously aware of at the time. I wouldn't say that my life had been purposeless before I met Suzanne, but it had lacked seriousness. I didn't feel intense excitement or commitment about anything – not my work, not my career, not even, initially, about Suzanne herself. I wanted the best for her, but I wasn't always interested in hearing her deepest feelings about life. The more she left me alone, the happier I was. I knew this irked her. She told me I had some wonderful qualities, but she wondered if I could make a true commitment to anything or anyone, including her.

Suzanne's illness made me throw down the gauntlet and take life on its own terms. The presence of mortality hitting me in the middle of life pulled forth in me a grit and determination not to drift into mediocrity. I became the sole support for someone who needed me and depended on me as no one ever had. In taking up the challenge, I learned more about myself than I ever thought possible. Fate turned me away from a carefree life and toward a life of purpose. I found a more strident voice. It pointed me in the direction of dedication and allegiance and entrusted me with the biggest enterprise I had ever undertaken.

By placing me at that party, fate made me responsible to an inner image of myself – one that I barely glimpsed at the time.

This was the same image that attracted Suzanne to me. She saw the companion she would need at her side when life threw its vicious curve. This interior image, I now believe, is what she responded to and what made her insist on leaving that party with me. And yet, I can also see the other sign of the coin. Perhaps this is a form of magical thinking. Perhaps the truth was more simple: A single woman in her late 30s, seeking to settle down, was aware of her power to engage me and see if I was someone who could be included in her world. Whatever the reasons, we evolved together into a future neither of us could have predicted. From the moment of her diagnosis, our love was focused on life and the present moment and also on the future and her death. I couldn't have imagined that years later the decision to end her life would rest in my hands.

 I remembered leaving the hospital after visiting her two weeks before her death. An incident captured my thoughts as I walked home. When I was two years old, I fell off the back of a bicycle that my older brother was riding. I split my chin on the curb, and my mother had to rush me to the emergency room at Morrisania Hospital in the Bronx, a few blocks from where we lived at the time. My chin was sutured and I was placed in the children's ward where I contracted an infection. As my fever rose and my condition worsened, the doctors, fearing for my life, placed me in isolation. Three weeks later, the infection was brought under control and a week after that, I was discharged. I couldn't then as a child have imagined the vitality and regeneration I took for granted. My cells were young, pluripotential, ready to begin the work of recovering, laying down new tissues effortlessly. My body programmed to cycle upwards towards the apex of growth and adulthood. With a disability the exact reverse is happening. The patient struggles valiantly against a force of gravity, which is always inexorably stronger, pulling them back like an undertow into the depths of the symptoms. And yet, one must not give up hope, even when all physicality is compromised, diseased, and at times appear doomed.

I thought further, had fate brought our two souls together? Could someone have looked in through the window of that children's ward in Morrisania Hospital at that 2-year-old with an infection raging through his body and foreseen his meeting and marrying, some 45 years later, a woman who would also contract an infection, in her case a fatal one – a woman who would become the love of his life?

Are the seeds of the future already planted at age two, or even, perhaps, before? Does an infant draw in with its first breath of life all the essential elements of its future life – what will give it joy and pain, command its devotion, ignite its love? Are all of these captured with the first intake of breath as if that first taste of the world contains, for each of us, all the world as we will know it?

Or was the confluence of those two infections mere coincidence? I continue to wonder about this as if it formed an essential foundation of the story of my life with Suzanne.

As we drove back to town after the funeral, the Sinatra classic, "Send in the Clowns," echoed in my head. I remembered a night in 1980 when Suzanne and went to Forest Hills Stadium to hear Frank Sinatra perform. I had loved Sinatra since I was a child of seven and heard him perform with Tommy Dorsey. My mother used to sing Sinatra songs while doing housework, and my brother and I gave each other his records and later his CDs as presents on birthdays and holidays. The lights dimmed, the stage went black and then a single klieg light floated over the vast stadium, filling it with a brilliant arc of yellow light. There was Sinatra, standing in an arrogant pose his hips thrust forward, a cigarette gracefully dangling from his sensuous lips. Waves of applause washed over him as he inhaled and let the smoke rise lazily from his mouth, swirling through the air. I remembered the heady mixture of man, music, and passion as Sinatra ignited the air with the first notes of, "Send in the Clowns": "Isn't it rich? Are we a pair – me with my feet on the ground, you in midair?" The spring air was filled with promise, his seductive voice crooning across a stadium of fans who spanned generations, all linked with the lyrics of romance, loneliness, and a bold defiance. The air crackled with possibility. Suzanne clasped my hand and her presence ran through my body like an electrical current. When Sinatra finished the song of longing and redemption, I turned to Suzanne. Her pale arms were swinging in rhythm to the memory of the music, refusing to acknowledge that the show was over. Her eyes were moist with emotion, fixed at the night sky draped over the stadium. "Oh God, I love this woman."

In those final days when she was unconscious and dying, I wanted her to send me a message through the fog of disease, a magical signal gleaming in her dark eyes, saying: Yes, disconnect all of this, I'm ready to go now. Please release me. Or: No, don't you dare. I want whatever time I have. I want to struggle on until the end, don't deprive me of each sacred second. After all I've always struggled, haven't I? Why should we expect it would be any different now at the end? But Suzanne never regained consciousness so I could imagine what her fingernails in my arm might have meant before she slipped into a void. The last words she spoke about being abandoned didn't indicate whether she was ready to surrender or wanted to continue to fight her way back for one last round. Suzanne had a Living Will and a Health Care Proxy which gave me the authority to make any and all health care decisions for her. It stated that she didn't not want cardiac resuscitation, mechanical respiration, artificial nutrition and hydration, antibiotics, transplants, oxygen therapy or blood transfusion. The document gave the agent, myself, the power to consent to her doctor not giving treatment or stopping treatment necessary to keep her alive

Harvey A. Kaplan

At the time we signed the Health Care Proxy, we never engaged in any intensive conversation about the full meaning of those words. Who could possibly realize what these words could ever come to mean in some future context. They were abstract concepts typed onto a legal document. Neither of us would not have wanted to be kept alive by artificial measures, however, we both knew at the time of signing that her physical condition was precarious. I couldn't bring myself to talk to her about the meaning of refusing life support care during the time of emergency, it was too naked an acknowledgement of the immanence of her death. At the point that she was already on life support, she never regained consciousness and so I couldn't ask her what she wanted to do. I could make the decision by myself.

When you first sign your Living Will the document is an abstraction, not linked with the stark reality when it is called into play with a radical immediacy. Years after the decision is made, when the living will is consulted, the conditions surrounding the implementation of it have often changed radically. The question moves away from the surreal issue of what happens if you were to die to the actuality that you are dying. In the end the terms and circumstances of her death confronted me alone, isolating me in a hospital room with a wall of medical professionals and forms and ethics committees all waiting for my decision.

When I recall peak moments with Suzanne, they resonate with feelings of contentment blending into sorrow, they surge and recede like strips of light arcing across waves of surf. The photograph of the young Suzanne, her olive shaped eyes gazing into the lens of the Polaroid on a distant afternoon of blazing summer against a backdrop of lush forest green is still scotchtaped to the refrigerator; a reprieve against days of physical misery, seizures and incontinence, hunting for a moment of peace like a treasure we hoarded against the hellish hours pressing in. The disease had burst Suzanne's pretty balloon, but beneath it lay a strong foundation made out of the smooth marble of her character that was endlessly willing to adapt. We consistently managed to love each other despite our human limitations.

As the MS progressed Suzanne suffered increasingly from seizures. They swept over her without warning, in the middle of a conversation she would bow down her head and evince a smile. In many of those instances, she lost all bladder control. When the seizures passed she would pick up her head and whisper to me what had occurred. Her smile was conspiratorial as she negotiated the sudden warm jet of urine dribbling down her legs. It was our secret. Her smile disguised the experience from other people. She surrendered to them and her ability to tolerate the physical vulnerability disguised the seizure in social situations. I was amazed at how well she could act through them as if she were being tickled. Her ability to cope with the impact of her physical disability was so impressive I joked with her that she could have been an actress.

How can I listen to Sinatra without her by my side? How can I hear his voice without calling her to mind? When I go to a restaurant that we both enjoyed or stroll down a path in the park where we once walked together, a spectral presence floats through my mind, a subtle wind of longing caresses my skin like an echo of Suzanne combing my hair with diligent tenderness. Now that she is gone, everything her soul imparted to me remains alive and sweeps the past and present into the future. I find myself crying as I walk through the sheep meadow, past Strawberry fields, and up past 72nd street past the block where John Lennon was shot. People gaze at me, an older man in a Burberry coat with tears streaming down my face, thinking I must be an eccentric, or I've gone off of an antidepressant. But their blur of compassionate curious faces can't grasp the peace that floats out through the fury and the mire of my veins with more potency than any drug.

Suzanne possessed a force that allowed me to throw off my inhibitions and plunge into the world of emotion, of gestation, of regeneration, of nightmares and caresses. In time I grasped that it was because that force, that courage, lay within me that she was able to inspire it and bring it out into the world without pettiness, deception, or the stranglehold of repression. In turn, I helped Suzanne surrender her ambivalence about marriage. Before she met me at that party she had several long relationships that had involved her deepest emotions, but she remained reluctant to consider the permanence and conventionality of the altar and commitment. The line of docile women with caged frustrated eyes like her mother's, the women counting linen and silverware and bemoaning their chipped porcelain as one might weep for a sudden bloody massacre in a third world country, haunted her. She chafed against the establishment and deliberately rejected the tedious conventional life patterned after her parents. In moving to New York City and then moving in with me, she learned that commitment could be unconventional and that stability was a form of transcendence, if we could both agree to create it.

It is daunting to be entrusted with another person's life. All relationships involve boundaries that determine how one cares for one's partner and what is permissible to say – what hopes and fears one may express. A child's caregiver knows that the child will eventually grow up and learn to fend for herself. As the child differentiates into maturity, the boundaries solidify and the relationship becomes more adult. This course is reversed when one cares for an adult with a degenerative disease: the boundaries become more fluid, rather than more solid. The progression of MS is insidious, reversing every developmental milestone that has established independence. One day the patient can't get up by herself. Weeks or months later, she can't turn over in bed. Still later she can't feed herself. Finally she lies like a helpless infant in a diaper waiting for strong competent hands to clean her from the sticky sensation of her urine or feces against her skin.

Who could have told me when I met Suzanne that I would be up for the task? Who could have known that I was capable of providing the strength and support necessary to sustain a relationship with such intense demands? When faced with serious illness or natural disasters, we are often far from the heroic. We burn with terror, fear, nightmares, inadequacies, and unresolved issues from earlier phases of life. But if we can embrace and understand these issues, we become more capable of heroism.

Consider a variety of inspiring lives. Johnny Cash became addicted to drugs, went to jail and experienced the haunting world of shadow bars of grim penitentiaries. But he translated trauma into art and recorded a live album at Folsom prison that far outsold the Beatles or the Stones, because it spoke directly to the primordial needs of his audience. Sigmund Freud suffered from hysterical symptoms, believed he was molested by his father and failed as a neurologist, but created a remarkable theory of the psyche that changed the world. Mother Theresa saw a homeless person die a horrible and needless death in the slums of Calcutta and devoted her life to creating a world with less poverty. According to Carl Jung, everyone is blessed with a heroic archetype that has the potential to transform darkness rather than run from it. As Hillman writes, "There is no mediocrity of character."

Chapter Four

The Party is Over

"My career is over," Suzanne announced one afternoon after she had gotten through another bout of pneumonia. She sat contemplating her hand, bruised from a fall two weeks earlier. The doctor had removed the white bandages as if he were cutting back a shroud to reveal purple blossoms of injured despairing flesh, as he reassured her that she would heal and was lucky it wasn't a fracture.

Her eyes were dark brown coals, smoldering with a soft sadness as she announced her recognition that after she was forced to give up her practice she had to carve out another path for herself in life. "And I had spent more than 10 years preparing for it. What should I prepare for now? I experience every decline of function as an interruption of my life." There was a mettle in her voice that intrigued me. Her career was up but I could sense that she was already planning something else.

In order to understand how other people dealt with MS Suzanne bought books to help her. Barbara Webster's *All of a Piece: A Life With Multiple Sclerosis* and Robert F. Murphy's *The Body Silent* were two of her favorites. Suzanne lay in bed, her face bathed in lamplight, transporting herself into other stories of people losing their mobility, their bladder control, their ability to breathe. Reading helped her feel that she was part of a community. It helped her understand her needs and fears, what she wanted from people, from me, and even from life.

> I would like to restore some order in my life. But it is so fragmented, and it is constantly being interrupted. It's hard to plan when I don't know how I will function next month, or even next week. I'm not even sure I want to keep my memories of my old life. They used to make me happy, now they give me a case of the blues. I've experienced such a break with the past, remembering it only makes me feel that I'm on the other side of things. It's like instead of rowing to the far side of a lake, you jump over it, and then you can't figure out how you got there.

Barbara Webster observes, "Disturbance of body image is very shattering. It disturbs the very experience and root of self." I recall a weekend trip Suzanne and I took in New Hope, Pennsylvania. After lunch we meandered through the town, looking in at shops and selecting a restaurant for dinner. Then we went back to our motel for a nap before washing up and going out for the evening. I heard Suzanne sobbing in the shower. This surprised me. We had both been happy just hours ago. Suzanne emerged from the bathroom, tears streaming down her face.

"This medication, this damned prednisone," she swore. "They claim it's a miracle drug, but look at what it's done to me. Would you just look?" She opened her terry cloth robe. I did my best not to turn away but for a second the revulsion flashed in my face and her eyes registered my naked emotion. She wept as I contemplated the collapsed contours of her frame. The curves and natural firmness that she had delighted in were lost in indistinct blobs of bloated, prematurely aged flesh. The medications had played havoc with her skeleton. Her bones seemed larger and awkward. Her body no longer fit on her frame. Her flesh twisted up like badly draped fabric.

"You won't have to take prednisone forever," I managed. "Don't you think your body will revert back to what it was?"

"No, it won't." Her voice was weak and far away. When she spoke her words were like bubbles emerging at the surface of the ocean, pockets of air that have traveled up from depths where light rarely penetrates. "From everything I've read, it's impossible to get back your shape once the drugs have taken effect. Besides, every time there's an exacerbation of the MS, I may have to go back on prednisone. So where does that leave me? I know I'm more than my body, but I'm also flesh and blood." Her arm leaned down on the sink and her back slumped down as if lifeless, her damp hair hanging down like strands of seaweed, obscuring her eyes.

"I know where it leaves me," I countered, squaring off to face her naked body. "I'm still in love with you, and I know what havoc all this is creating for you."

We didn't talk about it for the rest of the weekend, but when we got home, Suzanne found a photograph of herself, taken in the days when she was slim and healthy, and taped it to the refrigerator. She didn't harbor illusions that time would turn backwards and she would inhabit that model's body with high round breasts and graceful elegant legs like a Modigliani sculpture. She understood that she was being pulled by the dictates of the disease into a new body that mirrored her new life. The oncoming years were hurtling like a train gathering momentum, and that image was like a tree seen from a distant vista that was receding into the horizon forever. But the photograph helped her remember. It provided a vital continuity with her past. She mourned the loss of the way she once had looked and carried herself and all the pleasure she had derived from the long ago time when youth and vitality throbbed in her cells.

Most people tend to live life as if it is an unbroken series of events, moving from the past to the present and into the future. The truth is, we're always reinterpreting our lives. I see how my clients react when, during the course of therapy, they begin to realize how they have distorted their past, how they wasted time and missed opportunities they thought were beyond them, or grew up thinking they weren't loved or appreciated enough. When they gain insight into the ways they have misconstrued past events, leading to significant compromises in their lives and the consequent undermining of their happiness, they often experience periods of profound despair. Their psychological history has become discontinuous. As their perceptions of it change, they need to reconstruct different storylines in order to redefine the present.

MS runs different courses in different people. Neurologists now refer to it as the multiple scleroses, emphasizing how it is not one single illness but a myriad number of neurodegenerative diseases that resemble each other, like cousins. A severe disability creates a split between what went on before and what will follow. Physical damage has the power to sever the person from her past and to diminish a sense of self. The foundation you once thought firm is now shaky and unsteady. You have to live with this uncertainty for the rest of your life. It confronts you every day as you wake and get out of bed. It follows you through the day. You devise strategies to prevent it from dragging you into depression and withdrawal. Suzanne's photograph scotch taped to the refrigerator formed a bridge to an inner image of who she had been, of what her possibilities were like the desperate girl in a fairytale spinning gold out of her hair and providing a sense of an inviolable sense of possibility that gave her courage.

The manner in which we unfold our story is the way we come to experience life, and the way we imagine our life is the way we will continue to live it and depart from it. There are no naked events, plain facts, or simple data, only personal interpretations.

For Suzanne, dictating her observations into a tape recorder was a means of repairing the damage that had been done to her. In the telling of her story, she reaffirmed that her life was worth listening to. The afternoons of solitude and despair with the disintegration of her mind yawning before her like the jaws of a great devouring beast she found purpose in defining her existence, in coding a message that would let her voice echo in the universe forever. She needed to define what her body meant to her, and how she could reconcile all the changes it had been through, and essential part of her story was a story about the pressing needs of the body, its urgency, its fragility, its complex dictates. How was she to reconnect to this body that had undergone not only a crippling disability but also a double mastectomy?

Having a disability leaves no aspect of life untouched. But while there are losses, so also must there be gains. People with disabilities, or those who are chronically ill, can count as gains the development of closer relationships, deeper values, and a more urgent sense of the meaning of life. In *The Wounded Storyteller*, Frank writes, "Do not curse your fate; count your possibilities." The struggle becomes one of finding a place in the world to explore an altered course. In finding it, one can transform the entire idea of destiny.

Some writers use the term "illness" to express the experience of living through a disease. If disease relates to changes in the body, then illness relates to the fear and frustration of being inside a body that is caught in the turmoil of change. Suzanne's disability challenged every aspect of how she conceived of what her life meant. Losing her ability to function forced an existential centrality into the weave of the simplest moment. When Suzanne fumbled with the orange juice she wondered if there were a parallel universe where another version of herself existed, a robust healthier version that had been spared. When Suzanne camouflaged one of her seizures, she wondered if the nature of life was the savage laughter of black comedy. When the first symphonic storm of winter came she wondered if it would be her last, if the skeletal branches stretching out against the glacial lake mirrored her fate. Well intended friends advised her "to carry on as usual." But as she lost her career, her independence, her mobility, her figure, her motor coordination the question she struggled to answer was what could be gained from the experience, what could turn it from chaos into quest?

Psychotherapy at its core essence is the process of telling the therapist the story of your life. The therapist listens and, in the course of therapy, attempts to get the story told more coherently, until a final version emerges that is the best version you can tell. In *Tell Me A Story: A New Look at Real and Artificial Memory* (1983), Roger Schank discusses the need to tell our stories to others. He says: "We need to tell someone else a story that describes our experience because the process of creating a story also creates the memory structure that will contain the gist of the story for the rest of our lives." What he means is that filtering experience into the frame of a narrative allows us to store it in our memory banks for future use. We know that by having survived a harrowing struggle that we're stronger, and therefore able to better confront future ordeals. In this way, we create the memory of our illness for ourselves and give ourselves acknowledgement of our inner strength.

Through the stories we craft about ourselves, we emerge as full human beings, our characters are no longer our destinies, because we change them. We identify with what we have written in our narratives, producing threads that we draw on continually through the course of our lives. By confronting the truth in our life-stories, we acknowledge that our lives have not turned out as we may have wished, but that they were interrupted by this illness or that disability, and that we are limited in what we can do. Nevertheless, we affirm these limitations are real and simultaneously applaud what we are capable of discovering that adds novelty, that takes a strand of the thread and weaves the story into a tale of heroism rather than defeat.

To give voice to the narrative of your life honestly means to continue to live in the story, reflecting on it, musing over what you are becoming, so that you can make sense of a life that may seem to have reached an impasse. The history of an illness or disability often begins with devastation and destruction of the body. This violently interrupts the course of a life. The person becomes severed from his or her past, is transformed into someone else, – a patient, a victim, a sufferer, –and now the story must–if the person is to survive with hope–become one of transformation. The story requires the creation of psychological coherence out of biological incoherence. As I mentioned earlier, I am helping Suzanne write the story of her life, which she never wrote, and finish the story she never had a chance to complete.

Caregivers face many problems, including being peripheral to the main story, a spectator on the edge of a drama. We may feel that we are living solely for the other and that our lives have become over-burdened by sacrifice. Once the caregiver frames experience in this way, difficulties are inevitable. Living for the other may not be viable because of the overwhelming feeling of sacrifice. We need to redefine the relationship as having entered another phase. The challenge lies in surmounting the fear of the illness; in finding respect, concern, and a space for yourself to not be defined by the illness totally. Suzanne's parents couldn't find a way to re-frame the question in this way, but they were struggling to ask me if I could find a way to continue the story of infatuation with Suzanne to a stage of devotion. People with disabilities crave a caregiver who does more than help them with the tasks of daily living, but who is able to connect through listening, attending closely to what is being expressed. The caregiver listens to stories of incontinence, fatigue, memory loss, tremors and seizures, loss of control and almost unbearable frustration. Such stories are not easy to tell or to hear. A plateau is reached. The patient, caught in a web of symptoms, lives the same story over again like a frozen computer screen crashing, images going nowhere. Both the sufferer and the witness writhe in the inferno of a second act of a drama which can't resolve the tensions set in motion by the inciting incident of the sickness which pushed the story into motion. Then a factor in the relationship with illness transforms, without logic like a storm dissolving a high pressure system locked in over an oppressive sky. Through enough re-telling the boredom and stagnation pushes the person telling the story to convert the repetitive speech into an act of change which hurtles them to a new plateau where they confront the terms of change.

Suzanne spoke into her tape recorder about areas of life that most of us would rather not listen to. The story of a woman forced out of the period of her bloom too soon; withering in an accidental winter. After a period of adaptation to a new level of disability she would be subject to a sudden change, new symptoms entering and dragging her down.

The time is 1992. It's several years after we bought the condo and settled into the cozy rhythm of the lake. Cobalt blue in winter surrounded by naked trees and the white powder of snow. A languid green and cerulean in the summer when the trees filled with the miracle of leaves and the sky was filled with heat. One Saturday I told Suzanne that someone had given me a poster of Frank Sinatra and that she could see it when she came downstairs. She said that she would look at the poster before going downstairs. After a while, I went outside to see how she was and found her staring straight ahead, her eyes fixed on the lake.

"Are you okay?" I asked.

"No," she replied, turning to look at me. "It was hard for me to get down the stairs, and by the time I reached the bottom, my legs were giving out from under me, but I wanted to see your poster, so I went in and took a look. It's a great picture of him. I noticed the slogan: 'Sinatra: The Voice Forever.' Those words hit me like a blast of cold air. They made me think about myself, Harv. What is happening to my voice? I don't feel like myself when I talk. I don't feel as if I'm expressing who I am anymore. In fact, I don't know who I am. My whole existence has become vague and fuzzy. I need to find a different voice for myself. It can't be the same voice I had before this happened to me. It has to be a new one. Do you understand?"

I wanted to help her get this right. Good singers use their voices to convey the most complicated emotions and moods, especially when they talk of lost love, pain, and mourning. You can sense that they feel them as any gifted writer, artist, performer, or composer would feel them. Now Suzanne was talking about something I found hard to put my finger on. I listened, trying to distinguish whether this was one of the complex neuropsychiatric aspects of the illness or an existential crisis.

"Are you talking about your identity, or feeling like something physical is out of control?" I asked.

"No. I mean more than that. You know how many books I've read about MS, and how I've listened to what others say happens to them when the illness strikes. What I'm trying to say is I feel as if I don't recognize my own voice. First, I tend to slur my speech, but that's only part of it. I feel as if I say and do things I never used to. I smile at people when I don't feel like smiling. I need to reassure people that I'm okay and let them know they don't have to worry about me, but that doesn't feel real. It's not authentic. You keep doing this over a period of time and you wind up wondering who you are. It's more than what's happened to my body, that's only one part of it. It's not a false me, it's just a version of myself that's out of focus."

"That poster struck a chord. When I saw it, I said to myself, dammit, tell the world what you feel. But to tell the truth, Harv, I'm not so sure I'm in touch with what I feel. When I talk about my life or circumstances, I'm not sure who is doing the talking. I don't seem to know what this voice is expressing or what it is connected to. Do you have any idea what I'm talking about?"

"I think I do. In fact, I've been wondering why it seems harder and harder to engage you in serious discussions about your condition. It's as if you don't want to go there, to some deep feelings about yourself."

"No," Suzanne insisted, "That's not it. I think the voice that I've always depended on has somehow got lost, and I need to find it again."

I often wondered why Suzanne, and many other people with disabilities whom I've listened to, have so much trouble articulating their feelings about their illness, what it is doing to them, and their complicated reactions to it. This is their own personal drama, and they need to express it to the world. However, their voices, which should be vibrant, seem often to become muted and restrained when they approach the subject.

Suzanne's voice connected to her deepest emotions, how she experienced the changes in her life and the suffering and fears that MS brought into it. Desire means wanting more in life, and I saw how Suzanne's weakened body surrendered its desire. Did she have the right to act sexy, get angry, or be vulnerable? Why desire anything, what for? These questions presented a constant battle for her, but she fought it consistently, making sure that she her hair was cut, that she kept up her appearance, wore jewelry and nice clothes.

She confronted these truths about herself and the fact that her life could not turn out as she had hoped. Unlike a neurotic, where the tension is all intrapsychic, Suzanne's struggle pressed into the intensity of her own inner complexities about drive, desire and self perception but intensified by the experience of a radical loss of her bodily functions that were all encompassing.

They occurred at the period where most people are approaching the apex of their professional prowess. Increasingly, Suzanne realized that it was necessary to speak to me without worrying about my comfort level, even about the most profoundly disturbing sensations.

The hardest thing for her to acknowledge was her disappointment about friends and loved ones disappearing from her life. "I know they care, and a part of me understands that it's too hard for them to continue a relationship with me under the circumstances. I know I'm partially responsible. That it's me who has withdrawn from society." I often asked her why she didn't call the people she wanted to see.

"Kapp, you see I'm a coward in this way. I feel that I'm already falling apart and I can't risk the feeling of falling further if I call and then there's a moment when I detect their indifference or fear. Maybe it's a projection, but sometimes when I've called old friends to get caught up I hear a tentativeness on the other end of the phone. They can't come out and say it but I can feel it in their tone of voice, the artificial lilt of their laughter. It's their way of saying please, don't ask us for anything, please we're doing fine, please don't mess up our uncomplicated lives with a reminder that disease can rear it's ugly head and tear your world apart. It's nice to talk to you but we have to get going. That's what I hate most, the polite tension in their voices waiting to get off the phone, to be spared of me and my life."

Suzanne had no trouble finding her voice when it came to expressing her dismay at those doctors who were rude or dismissive toward her, or at me when I didn't treat her well. I knew she was always right in these instances and was glad that she trusted me enough to speak her truth. After I bought her a tape recorder she spent afternoons pressing the button and talking into the microphone, drifting in and out of consciousness.

Harvey A. Kaplan

On good days there were at least two cassettes neatly boxed with her scrawled barely legible handwriting on the labels in colored markers. On bad days the tape recorder lay untouched and she would lie prone, stroking herself absently, dialing friends only to find that her fingers couldn't work the dial pad and she was leaving messages for total strangers.

But over time the piles of cassettes by her tape recorder grew higher.

> If you don't look good to yourself, how can you imagine that you might look good to someone else? You pass a mirror and don't like what you see. Is it any wonder that you soon fall into a negative and pessimistic state of mind? Maybe you feel that you have been cheated in life, that you've been denied certain rights that others take for granted. You see people walking, running, playing tennis or biking, their bodies responding to their will, their smiles reflecting the satisfaction they take in their appearance and performance. And what do you feel? Perhaps envy–you can't do the physical things they do. Maybe a feeling of deep melancholy comes over you, but you don't want pity, so you put on a happy face to show that you can live with your situation.

But what happens when you arrive at a point in life when every hour is heavy with the desire to be returned, with minimal struggle, into the simple pleasure of oblivion? A brown withered leaf slips effortlessly from the tree branch into the coming of the winter solstice, the triumph of night.

Chapter Five

These Foolish Things Remind Me of You

Robert Louis Stevenson once remarked: "Life is not so much a matter of holding good cards, but sometimes playing a poor hand well." When disability befalls us how do we find the strength and resilience to combat it? How do we find the courage to try to beat the odds? And what does it take to play our hand as well as we can? And what does it mean to throw in our hand? The questions of active and passive euthanasia surges with a life of its own, insisting on consideration everywhere in the media of the moment; the academy award winning film, Million Dollar Baby, in the true-life story of Terri Schiavo, which held the world captive for months. These stories kept me company, mirrors of the solutions to protracted life in a vegetative state that beckoned on movie screens, in the tabloids, in heated discussions on talk shows and in the wake of Suzanne's death, I was less alone.

Mercy killing and physician assisted suicide has been considered from multiple angles, praised by some and attacked on moral grounds by many religious groups. After seeing Million Dollar Baby I considered the mercy killing that took place in that film and story as a moral outcome. Maggie Fitzgerald, the prizefighter who rises up from dirt to the championship against all odds, sustains a severe blow in the ring that leaves her a quadriplegic. The final act of the film pushes beyond the boundaries of the usual major studio sentimentality. Maggie loses a leg and begs to be allowed to die. When no one assists her, she uses the only power that she has, biting her tongue to attempt to suffocate on her own blood, but this fails. Paralyzed and helpless in her hospital bed, she is trapped in an existence she can't bear, unable to kill herself. Ultimately, Frankie Dunn, her trainer, sneaks into her hospital room and injects adrenaline into her feeding tube, which triggers a stroke and kills her and then disappears like a phantasm, hovering over a tiny diner where Maggie had once found solace.

People who support this kind of euthanasia argue that relief of suffering is the primary motivation and that it is an option only for those who request it. People who oppose this option claim that society has no right to take a human life under any circumstances, no matter how heinous.

In the last days, standing at the hospital bed, watching Suzanne fight against her tubing, I remembered her in a white sweater during the first years of our marriage, the powerful arc of her arm wielding a tennis racket, her pride in her perfect serve, the ball slicing the air. Suzanne lounging in a red sarong on the cliffs of Santorini, drinking a glass of grappa, her teeth glistening white against her tanned skin. Then Suzanne stumbling up the stairs at the condo, frozen, shivering like a child, putting her fingers into her mouth and chewing her nails to relieve the nameless dread of not knowing who she was, of words floating like a distant mysterious necklace of meanings beyond her comprehension.

I wrestled with the question of whether her life had already been taken. At times it seemed it was obvious that the demon had finally triumphed, and the woman lying flaccid and motionless with an oxygen tube was finally vanquished, devoid of life. Her glassy eyes fixed at the ceiling seemed to have already abandoned this world. And yet it had been only fourteen days earlier that we had surged with hope from the new surgery, contemplating our life by the lake, and the possibility of a few last few years that seemed somehow promised to us. Could that have vanished permanently. The doctors were unified in their tribe of white that it had. Yet the ultimate decision to disconnect her life support rested on me. Had they not started it in the first place, they stated they would not do it now. But given that it was already in place but proving to be useless in curing her, the decision rested on me and a complex circuit of ethics committees.

In Million Dollar Baby, the edgy cynical Frankie is depicted as a courageous man who takes an extreme personal risk to ease another's suffering. Yet, he does kill Maggie and sneaks away. Whether he couldn't bear to see her remain alive in a tormented parody of her former life is a question that receded against her consciously expressed conception of her own life as having ended and her desperation to be released into a dignified death?

For Frankie it was easier. His beloved had bitten off her tongue, she had begged him to release her. A suppressed sexual tension permeated the atmosphere of the film as she rose to stardom in the boxing world, with the lingering question of whether Frankie would become her lover or remain in the role of a paternal mentor. The script didn't succumb to the cliché of allowing them to fall into a romance and a way to live happily ever after. Having accepted her invitation to be inducted into the violent world of boxing, he eases her away with a swift painless injection.

I sat watching the film weeping, hiding my face in my hands, embarrassed that I would be seen in the darkness of the theater. I wanted to hide, but the theatre was crowded. I remained trapped and motionless, staring at my lap. The protests spawned by the film were fast and inevitable. Marcie Roth, of the National Spinal Cord Injury Association, believed the movie advanced an alarmist agenda and presented distorted interpretations of disability. In New Mobility (April 2005), she observed: "Any movie that sends a message that having a spinal cord injury is a fate worse than death is a movie that concerns us tremendously." But she missed the point. The problem isn't with a spinal cord injury, it's with the loss of the purpose of life that's been disconnected from drive and desire. Does existence attached to tubes and wires constitute life itself or is it a simulacrum of existence extended by tricks of technology.

At the end of Suzanne's life the problem was not that Suzanne lacked consciousness to make any decision on her own. She was going to die from an infection in the course of the next several weeks or months, and it was impossible to predict just how long multiple antibiotics and oxygen might continue to allow her to linger in this state. The question was now whether I should take action to take the artificiality out of the process, to allow nature to accelerate unimpeded, to return Suzanne into the last final snowstorm without the impedance of medical technologies that continued her biological existence but without any quality of life.

Twenty-five years ago Karen Quinlan collapsed at a party after having mixed alcohol with tranquilizers. Her life was saved, but she suffered brain damage and lapsed into what doctors call a "persistent vegetative state." Her family waged, and ultimately won, a public legal battle for the right to remove their daughter's life support system. But, in an outcome that surprised everyone, Karen Ann kept breathing after her respirator was disconnected. She remained in a coma for almost 10 years until her death in 1985. I recalled as a psychology intern working at a nursing home in the North Bronx that smelled of detergent and fungus, the ward for the comatose. Loyal families came in daily with gifts and flowers, some even had the comatose family member propped up with televisions and radios. They whispered to them. They prayed over their inert bodies, rolling their eyes heavenwards. They brought daily offerings of candies and ice cream. They believed that if their devotion to their comatose loved ones was firm and without hesitation they would bring them back, awakening from the dark sleep that trapped them. Who is to say that they are wrong? Perhaps for them this is a truth worth living by. That afternoons of whispered prayers and bouquets of delphiniums wrapped in colorful paper is their form of honoring life and the comatose cannot raise their hands in a final farewell and insist on being allowed to exit the stage.

But there never has been any real challenge to the basic tenet set forth in the Quinlan ruling: A patient has a right to refuse life-prolonging treatment, and that right reverts to a designated family member if the patient is no longer able to speak for himself or herself.

In 1990 Terri Schiavo sustained severe brain damage after having been deprived of oxygen. Her devoted followers, many of whom were seen as a spiritual life-support network, kept a constant vigil outside her hospital, praying that she would be kept alive and that the life-sustaining feeding tube would not be removed. Although brain-damaged, she could breathe on her own, but needed nourishment to continue living. Her family claimed that she had conscious awareness of her surroundings and that she made token responses to their appearance. Her husband disagreed and insisted that she be removed from life-support. Congressman Tom Delay took up the protest. After the family lost their case in court, President Bush signed a bill, rushed through by Congress, in a last-ditch effort to restore her feeding tube.

Some thought that, given proper treatment, there was no reason Terri Schiavo could not live out her life. Watching her on television I experienced the eerie impression that she possessed some degree of consciousness. Even as the doctors concurred that she was brain dead, I wanted to believe that part of her lived, mesmerized by her honest, pure face that reminded me of the simplicity of milk, gazing up at the camera with translucent innocence. Terri continued in this persistent vegetative state, which some came to view as a saintly one, for 15 years, while the feud continued between her husband, Michael, who argued for Terri's right to die with dignity, and Terri's parents and brother and sister, who fought to sustain her life.

In a March 31, 2005, interview on National Public Radio's "All Things Considered," Dr. Jay Wolfson, a professor of public health at the University of South Florida, and Terri's court-appointed guardian, said that the most disconcerting thing for him was in spending time in her room. "I would sit with her sometimes for hours, holding her hand, holding her head in my hand, stroking her hair, talking to her. I played music for her. I desperately wanted her to give me some consistent indication that she was interacting and responsive, and I was unable to observe or elicit any trace of response."

Terri's husband noted that after attending funerals of family members who had been on artificial life support before they died, Terri told him that she would never want to live connected to a tube. This, and Michael's status as Terri's husband, served as the basis for the ruling that allowed the feeding tube to be removed.

I wondered if I took Suzanne off the respirator whether it would rescue her soul or extinguish it forever. Was my own narcissism playing a role in my desire to end her life, a different version of lifting her from the chair by her hair because I couldn't bear my own helplessness? Was it my own unresolved impatience surging forward to see the curtain fall, to have everything fall into an order fashioned by my own hand, against all odds, and perhaps against the wishes of the silent sleeping woman who I had loved for thirty years?

Chapter Six

Memories of You

Normally, the immune system acts as a defense, combating bacteria, viruses, funguses and other pathogens that invade the body. The immune system includes an elaborate network of white blood cells, responsible for identifying and destroying harmful invaders. In an autoimmune disease, these cells mistakenly identify the body's own tissues as foreign invaders. The body turns against itself. I would lie next to Suzanne, feeling my own body pulsing with vitality and health. I went to a gymnasium. I lost weight. I could feel blood and life coursing through my veins effortlessly. I would stroke her gently, like a beloved cat, feeling the flaccidity of her muscles beneath my hand, sensing the way her flesh was inert and unresponsive, trying to will a current of life energy into her by osmosis.

In MS, the immune system attacks the "white matter" which consists of nerve fibers that transmits signals throughout the body. This attack results in the formation of lesions and a loss of myelin – a white, fatty material that encloses certain nerve fibers. MS erodes the covering around the myelin sheath and thus disrupts signals between the brain and the body. This nerve damage causes all kinds of symptoms. MS disrupts many bodily function, including sight, speech, gait, mobility, bladder and bowel functions, and cognitive skills. Sometimes she would plead with me, ashamed of her need, but determined that her voice be heard. "Please Harv, just a glass of water." "Please Harv, just a little more chocolate." "Please, please, please." And I would bring her what she wanted and held her in my arms, imagining my hands spread like wings, flying us away from the warfare and erosion of her doomed body.

The medical establishment currently believes that certain patients have a genetic predisposition toward MS, but they don't necessarily develop the disease unless some environmental factor triggers it. Research has shown a significant, though not conclusive, correlation between smoking and MS. Suzanne had been a smoker earlier in her life and, even during our marriage, she would revert back to the habit when under stress, then quit, then start again only to quit once more. Sometimes in the darkness, before she drifted into sleep, she would remonstrate, "I should never have smoked. Perhaps I did this to myself. If only there were a reason, if there was something I can understand or give back to the world." Her eyes were dark flashing stones in her pale face in the lamplight. "You know that Sinatra sang, the one that goes 'I ate it up and spit it out?' I don't want to spit something out but I want to spit something back. Something that can make sense of this whole experience, that would make me feel like I had a purpose."

"Use the tape recorder, you'll have enough there to write a book."

In most patients, MS initially follows a relapsing-remitting course with acute attacks followed by full or partial recovery. The majority of people who begin with the relapsing-remitting course eventually develop a Secondary Progressive course, and disability increases over time, with or without actual acute attacks. Suzanne was unfortunate. Her MS followed the usual course from relapsing/

remitting to Secondary Progressive. It is currently not understood why the disease converts to Secondary Progressive MS in some people and not in others. All patients ultimately encounter problems with motor skills, especially in their legs. Some go blind. Others experience uncontrollable tremors, others only slight ones. Some retain upper body coordination, enabling them to write and use their arms even when they can no longer walk; others lose the use of all four limbs. Some people experience only minor fatigue. "It's strange," Suzanne often remarked. "I know I've been dealt a shitty hand, and I'm trying to do what I can with it, but the problem is I don't know what hand it is. I don't know what ace fate may throw me, or if all the cards are a losing streak. There are some things you just can't know no matter how hard you try."

MS is infinitely more subtle than a heart attack, stroke or cancer. Suzanne wasn't abruptly paralyzed or demented. Her losses accrued gradually over a period of 19 years. She was spared the sudden, drastic trauma of a car crash or a massive stroke. Nonetheless, the physical and psychological effects were profound in a different way. Multiple sclerosis was a presence living with us, making us reconsider everything from the way we made love to what we put in our retirement accounts. As adults we all understand that we are going to die. But this truth remains an abstraction for most of us until our last decade of life. In the meantime, existing in a realm of relative health, our minds are not focused on morbidity and mortality, we imagine our deaths as an abstraction in a fantasied future that will occur naturally, in our beds, after our lives are lived to completion. Suzanne was reminded every day of the reality of how fragile her life was, how easily it could end, and how the quality of it could hit a sudden new negative plateau of erosion. We tried to remain on the course of a quest narrative, but at times we would both be overwhelmed by a new crisis; urine dribbling around her legs as she tried to negotiate her scooter down the aisles of a supermarket; medications causing visual hallucinations, armies of insects swarmed before her vision as she tried to rest; at times she thought she saw ghosts in the steam rising out of the tea kettle. Suzanne opened the cupboard and realized that all of our wedding china was gone, that over the course of years the tremors in her arms had caused her to drop all of the plates and glasses and now none of the original set were left. At those moments the chaos narrative returned and existence was populated with devouring monsters.

We continued finding the rhythm between the Monday to Friday workweek and the pleasure of the weekends in nature, knowing that a mysterious and destructive process was unraveling Suzanne's brain. At first we couldn't see the disease except as the white fuzzy patches on her CAT scan, but we knew it lurked like a shark beneath the surface of a tranquil sea. Then the shark took our lives between its teeth and shook us with great violence – leaving professional plans, familial relationships and ideas of mortality floating disemboweled in the bloody water until the attack receded and clarity returned. But we couldn't know when the ominous dorsal fin would return and we couldn't give in to the impulse to swim towards it and surrender: devour me already, just end this process, you're going to win in the end.

"It's awful not being in control of your body, but it's my mind that I worry about most," Suzanne sighed, one languid August afternoon as we sat watching geese flying over the lake. She had been happy that morning and then the happiness had evaporated without warning, leaving her voice flat. "It's like this disease has a mind of its own, and despite all the treatments and interventions, it will do what it wants to me."

"I feel so frustrated when I can't do the smallest things," she observed. "Like write a name in my telephone book or dial a phone number. I even have trouble remembering what we talked about yesterday."

"But it may get better. You're doing all you can."

"I know." An uneasy silence filled the condo. I pulled the drapes and looked out across the gray sky, pregnant with the coming rain. That afternoon we drove through the downpour to a movie, we ate pizza, and drank wine and pretended for a moment that we were college kids celebrating after a final exam. We made love with an added spark of intensity, driving the shadow of the disease away with the friction between our bodies.

The shark did not swim away as we had hoped. Small, silent increments of weakness erupted into major changes in function, as Suzanne's MS progressed from the relapsing-remitting course to one of steep decline. Prednisone, a steroid she took to combat inflammation in her joints, caused her to gain a tremendous amount of weight and eventually caused her shoulder bones to deteriorate. Fatigue reduced her to almost total inertia. She progressively lost mobility, beginning with a limit on the distance she could walk and ending with her confinement in a wheelchair. After ten years she lost the ability to feed herself and turn over in bed.

As time progressed, the flare-ups of MS left increasing residual damage. There were fewer afternoons spent at the movies, fewer evenings of making love and forcing the despair into the distance with the pleasure that rose up between us. In the remission phase she never regained her lost functions. When she put her arms around me, the tremors made it impossible for her to hug me. When she kissed me, her lips twitched and she grew dizzy. We had two friends from the Freudian Society who suffered from the disease. Initially Suzanne's course seemed more benign. She was able to walk and carried herself with greater balance. We both thought that this was such a good omen for the future. But as it turned out, our friends had a different progression of the MS, and over time they retained clearer cognitive functioning, while Suzanne's functioning declined with increasing speed.

I stopped saying, "It may get better, you're doing all you can."

Suzanne's vision blurred, she was overwhelmed with a general lack of coordination between her two eyes. Her muscles shriveled, her speech slurred, she was flooded with involuntary contraction of her muscles and numbness and loss of sensation in certain parts of her body. Her coordination and balance declined until she couldn't stand at all. She lost her sexual arousal, not only from her struggles with her body falling apart, but from a deep switch in her brain that the disease turned off, that made it impossible to desire anything. As the years continued she slept most of the day, due to the side effects of her countless bottles of medications. In the final years she suffered from severe decline in her cognitive functioning. She would flicker back into consciousness for an hour or too and then become confused by the plots of soap operas or the unfolding of current events.

When she could no longer stand up, she stopped wearing underwear, because it was too difficult for me or her caregiver to hold her up while pulling down her panties so she could relieve herself.

In Suzanne's own words, her greatest challenge was the persistent, overwhelming fatigue:

> If it weren't for this awful fatigue I think I could manage . So much of me has been taken away like my writing, our long discussions, my talks with colleagues. Now I hardly talk to anyone but you and Mana. All that I could get around, I think, but not the fatigue. I don't want to sleep what's left of my life away.

Patients with MS tire because the demyelinated nerve fibers are forced to use more energy to conduct impulses to the brain. Thus fatigue sets in more rapidly than it does with healthy fibers. The weakened muscles rely on stronger ones, which, in turn, tire faster. A person suffering from MS requires two to three times the energy that an able-bodied person uses to walk a single block. In the beginning of her illness, Suzanne could walk fine for a block or two, then she developed a slight limp. The further she walked, the more pronounced the limp became. Soon one leg would drag, then the other, and finally, both legs stopped working altogether.

I often wonder how she could have tolerated this invasion and relentless destruction of her body. Ironically, the cognitive impairments may have helped her cope with this devastation. She would lapse into a dreamlike condition fueled by medication. She sometimes became quiet, sweet and almost infantile. At other moments she lapsed into a complete state of total withdrawal, a blankness like a living death. I would mutter a quiet prayer, as I held her unresponsive hand. "Oh please, Lord, don't leave her this way."

I used to track her medications, giving myself work that provided the illusion that something could control this. Her prescription drugs included Neurontin, which alleviates pain from nerve dysfunction, Amantadine, to fight the fatigue, and Detrol to counter the urinary incontinence, Klonopin to alleviate spasticity. I remember Lenore, one of her first caregivers, filling up a plastic pillbox with tablet after tablet increasing in complexity, placing them into Suzanne's passive mouth, across an endless parade of days. I was lucky to have an insurance policy from the Board of Education, which paid for most of it. She took large amounts of pills in the morning, afternoon and in the evening. Wherever we went, the first thing we did was make sure that she had all her "meds" as she called them. She became terrified if one of the bottles were misplaced or short of tablets. She was most frightened of the seizures. There was no controlling them, and they could pounce upon her without any advance warning. An uncontrollable anxiety, a mounting nameless terror accompanied her like a second skin. She dictated into the tape: "If you can't feel safe within your body where can you feel safe?"

For a time Prozac revived her ebullience and equilibrium. I used to regard advertisements for antidepressants with skepticism. Slender happy Americans, often blonde women, depicted in dark indigo rooms transformed into creatures of fire in a blaze of glossy color, streaming out into the world ready to shop and copulate. Prozac gave Suzanne a respite from the incessant ocean of blackness, the endless struggle against the stark reality of permanent decay. Antidepressants extended the length of time she could practice psychotherapy. I'm not sure what it was that led Suzanne to discontinue her practice. She believed strongly in using counter-transference – her own emotional reactions to her patients – as a therapeutic tool. As her MS progressed, we feared that her concern over her health and the side effects of medications might impair her ability to listen closely. At length, we agreed that it would be best for her to discontinue her practice altogether. This was another eerie milestone.

When Suzanne started slurring her speech, she became self conscious about talking in front of people. This increased her social isolation but she pressed on to attend parties although it was difficult to maneuver her wheelchair through a crowd. Her arms were no longer strong enough to move her wheelchair by herself, so she had to remain wherever I parked her. She could not choose her own company, but had to wait for others to approach her. People tend to stand up at parties to socialize, but to talk to Suzanne they had to sit down next to her. Often, she was ignored until someone realized she needed someone to get her a plate of food or something to drink. People were more than happy to do this, and Suzanne allowed it. But she couldn't bear feeling useless and uninteresting.

Initially Suzanne had reacted to the MS better than I did. "It's not my fault that I have this disability," she said. But over time she feared that others found her less interesting than she had been. Consciously or unconsciously, many people avoid the sick and disabled, because they don't want to look at the possibility that illness may erupt into their lives. Suzanne hadn't kept up with the psychoanalytic literature, so she found herself uninteresting. Her slurred speech made it difficult for her to express herself. Ultimately, she gave up going to large social gatherings. "It's just too hard," she complained. While many associates sent their regards through me, she sensed that they pitied her. The remnants of a healthy pride would not allow her to be the object of someone's pity.

As she lost the ability to write, she increased recording her feelings and experiences on tape:

> I remember telling Harv that it was getting too hard for me to dress in the mornings to see my patients. I found it draining and felt that the medication I was taking was diminishing my ability to listen to the patients' problems. Harv told me that he had similar thoughts, but didn't feel comfortable bringing them up to me. He told me that he would support me in this, and that we could handle it financially. Caroline had finished college and my salary was no longer essential.
>
> I felt awful, yet, in some ways was relieved not to have this worry hanging over me anymore. I gave six months' notice to my patients and that September, stopped practicing. The relief did not last long, for then I came face to face with the question, "Who are you, now?" At age 49, what was I to do with my life? I knew I did not want to make Harv the center of it or to have to rely on him to fill my days.

49 is an age when many people experience a midlife crisis that inspires them to take on new hobbies or change careers. But at 49, the realities of Suzanne's disability were bleak. She couldn't become a filmmaker or start a business from home when she could barely button her blouse.

Suzanne once asked me how I viewed her usefulness in life, now that the career, which she had worked so hard to establish, was over. As I wrote this memoir, I understood the full impact that discontinuing her practice had on her. Prior to Suzanne's illness, we had gone to psychoanalytic meetings, conferences, and lectures together on a regular basis. At home in the evenings, we endlessly discussed theories of development, pathology, perversions, all the tyrannies and triumphs of the mind in its baroque complexity. We debated topics such as whether guilt and envy were the true motivators of creativity and how a theory of Eros could explain the Holocaust or the suicide of Sylvia Plath. Our entire lives were organized around psychoanalytic inquiry and trying to understand the roots of human behavior. The meanings of our dreams and our patients. My recurring dream of riding in night train across the black skies of Central Europe always waking up before the vision of the gentle alps sloping down to the Mediterranean. The dreams of images, a glinting silver car stopping in a dark woods in the middle of snow and a blonde woman with hair like Dominique Sand drawing her fingers down the glass, the sensation of clawing against impossible odds before waking up, an act of sacrifice and heroism that was uncompleted. As Suzanne became lost in the fog of disease I went to conferences and lectures without her. She would wave me on from the door. "Go on, you need a life, I'll be fine, just report back. I've got my music to listen to." She'd manage a smile as she guided her wheelchair to the stereo. She filled the house with Dvorak, the fury of Beethoven, the darkness of the late Liszt, the harmonies of the Beatles.

As her illness progressed, most of her professional friends drifted away. At the beginning, they rallied around her, but as it became more difficult for her to go to meetings and enter into the politics of the New York Freudian Society, where she had long been a respected member, they gradually dropped out of sight. To some extent, this was Suzanne's doing, because she seldom invited them to visit and rarely called them if they did not phone her. Her illness required people to develop a new language with which to speak of the terms of erosion. It required a new code of learning how to address her without self consciousness, overcoming the awkwardness and uncertainty of not knowing what her slurred speech or sudden erratic loss of postural tone meant. As hard as she tried to minimize the distress she was in, Suzanne was aware she had entered a different world of an underwater consciousness, a language of fatigue. And part of her did not want to face the arduous climb back up to the surface where her colleagues splashed around with ideas and theories and ideas for conferences and vacations. Over the years her self-image became drastically altered, her identity became hazy. Freud wrote, "The ego is first and foremost a body ego." As the body begins disintegrating, the ego's ability to maintain a core sense of self stalls out like a car in the wrong gear, climbing an impossible road of ice. It was disorienting for her to find herself separated from professional interests she once had pursed with such passion and from so many people she had once so enjoyed being with. She used to think of herself as a person of intelligence and substance, now she was feeling somewhat worthless and had to battle her increasing despair. It was a catastrophic transformation; not only was her body altered, but her way of thinking about herself was profoundly disrupted.

As Suzanne's husband, at times I became a hostage to the disease, locked in a closet while she was out in the arena with terrorists subjecting her to a slow, deliberate torture. The doctors kept advising that all we could do was wait, remain optimistic but at the same time to be realistic. I still don't know what that means. I tried to separate the hyperbole of saying, "It will be all right," from the truth that permeated the antiseptic smells of the clinical examining rooms. It was obvious that it was not going to be all right. We learned to walk a strange balance between being optimistic and grim. We made a commitment to live in the moment, unsure how long the moment would last. We procrastinated less. We made each day a celebration. We also realized that we did not have forever to say the things we meant to say.

As colleagues withdrew, so did Suzanne. She lost interest in maintaining a social life. Facing the world each day became an ordeal of medication regimens, tremors, incontinence, unexpected symptoms of vertigo, and the disconcerting feeling that she could no longer trust her own perceptions. She struggled not to turn her back on the world, not to give into the debilitating exhaustion that plagued her and made her want to crawl back into bed and pull the covers over her head, but there were days when she lost the struggle. Regression is inevitable as the body loses functional capacities. Our bodies give us a sense of our ability to plan, master, execute plans, consolidate reality; our bodies give us our sense of self. The disease was forcing her to be a conventional, dependent woman – so different from free spirit filled with wanderlust who immersed herself in German culture and language. "I used to be such an independent person," she observed. "Now I am brought back under my husband's protection and must rely on him for almost everything. I'm worse than a 1950s housewife. I'm not just losing my autonomy, but also my self-worth."

She recorded the following on tape:

> I knew I had to find some solution to this sense that I was losing my identity. It seemed I was becoming faceless and going nowhere. Emotional pain was a constant. Only by thinking of nothing could I feel nothing. Certainly this was preferable to thinking of what lay ahead. I stopped reading the MS newsletters and the articles about people who were making great strides in their emotional battle with MS. Maybe they didn't suffer the same fatigue that I did, or maybe they had a rosier outlook on life. I wanted to keep my feelings secret. I didn't even want to talk about them to Harv or to friends who also had MS. I knew I had to come up with some idea about how I was going to live my life. I couldn't stay in this stupor forever. How could I define myself and give myself some reason for living out my life?

Seven years into the illness Suzanne had withdrawn into a small circle of close personal friends whom she had known for many years and who were more at ease with her disability. People outside this circle could not adjust to what had happened to her. When

I saw colleagues at meetings, they would dutifully ask me how Suzanne was, and I would say, "Hanging in." A few would press me for details, but most did not want to know more than that. I grew to understand it. This was not their story. They had their own lives, concerns, children, sick relatives of their own.

A disabled person needs to join a different tribe – to find others who are dealing with disability, who understand, who do not find the experience a foreign language they cannot speak. Suzanne befriended other people with disabilities, one of whom lived in our building. She also joined a neighborhood support group. This provided support for some years but there was a time as the disease progressed when she lost interest in attending even those meetings.

I reflect on key milestones: buying the condo, ending her practice, redefining her social circle, and finally withdrawing into a state of greater isolation. As I pushed Suzanne's wheelchair down the street, people would smile and greet her as if she were a child. The artificial kindness and contrived condescension irked me. Suzanne greeted them warmly and smiled back. I wanted her to take more exception to being treated like a child, but an innate sweetness emerged from deep within her and she handled it with grace. Perhaps this is part of Suzanne's unspoken legacy as I reflect back on it. She could face the endless parade of masked faces twisted into condescending socially appropriate smiles concealing their relief that this image of a wrecked woman would never be them. Suzanne smiled back, turning her head to look when she could, her eyes reaching out through the layers of medication and her disability burnt away and became meaningless as a common ground of humanity flickered between them.

Throughout her illness, Suzanne's face retained the contours of her regal nose. Her large brown eyes, and thick, rolling black hair were not ravaged by the onslaught of illness. Her small white sculpted ears adorned with sapphires remained unchanged. Before the MS, she had prided herself on her body and the vivacious energy that drew people to her. As her illness progressed, she came to view her body as her enemy. Something she once loved, she now resented. "You can't send your body away," she observed. "It's attached to you. Mine is like some outside force that has been brought in specifically to exert damage."

Simone de Beauvoir wrote that the body is not a thing, an entity separate from the mind and from the rest of the world. The body is also a set of relationships that link the outer world and the mind into a system. When this system is disrupted, a sense of disorientation sets in. Yet as serious as her illness became and in all the years that she struggled with it, she refused to see herself as a victim. She was much too smart for that and, hard as it may be to believe, she was not bitter over her fate. She knew that for the first forty-five years of her life she had everything going for her. Her life was privileged, she lived it to the fullest, and that made it easier to bear what came later.

In our relationship, Suzanne maintained a ready sense of humor and used it to overcome feelings of hopelessness. I remember once when we had been out for a drive and I pulled into a gas station to fill up the tank. On impulse, I decided to wash the windshield. I sponged the window, then took the squeegee to wipe off the excess water. From her front-seat vantage point, Suzanne raised her feeble hand, indicating a missed spot. I kept working with the squeegee and she kept using her index finger to pointing out missed spots, because her arm had gone flaccid at the elbow. I diligently attacked each spot she pointed to. Suzanne, smiling innocently the whole time, kept finding more missed spots and pointing out each one. Finally, she stopped, and I walked back to my side of the car. Just as I was about to open the door and get in, she shook her head, beckoned me back, and pointed out another spot I had missed.

Saving Beauty

But outside the circle of our closest friends, humor didn't always work. Suzanne was often at a loss as to how to respond to the indifference or impatience of friends. She couldn't turn on her heel and walk away. She worried about offending people and driving them out of her life forever, so she bottled up her emotions and wore the mask of a smile. This alienated her further from the robust person she once had been, that feisty woman who never missed a chance to stand up her herself.

Sometimes Suzanne compared her plight to that of a prizefighter:

> I feel like a boxer who's pounded mercilessly, round after round. But after twelve or fifteen rounds, a boxing match ends. For me, the match will never end. Except in one way, and I'm afraid to discuss that, even with you. … This enemy inside me is invisible. I know I'd have the guts to kill it, if only I could see it. What will the end look like? Will the wreckage continue until I can no longer breathe?

In *The Body Silent* (1987) Robert F. Murphy makes this cogent observation about people with disabilities:

> They are afflicted with a malady of the body that is translated into a cancer within the self and a disease of social relationships. They have experienced a transformation of the essential condition of their being in the world. They have become aliens, even exiles, in their own lands.

At the time he wrote this, Murphy knew he had an inoperable tumor. He wrote this book, filled with brilliance, as his life ebbed away from him. Likewise, Suzanne recorded her thoughts in her tape recorder, as she redefined her connection to the world:

> I sometimes think of death as preferable, but if Harv is willing to help me and continue to support me, it's worth my effort to

go on fighting. Would I really be better off dead? No, I don't think so because I truly celebrate life, looking at another day, another flower, looking forward to hearing another song. Every weekend, Harv puts on Jonathan Schwartz and plays the songs he loves by Frank Sinatra and Tony Bennett. I love those songs, too, maybe more for sharing them with him. I feel close to Harv when we listen to Sinatra. I know he wants me to love this music as much as he does, yet my true musical love is opera. Only with opera can I feel the excitement in the music and the singing.

But sharing things is so important to Harv that I even look forward to hearing him ask me every Sunday night, as I know he will: "What do you want for dinner?" Of course I give him the answer he's expecting: "What about Chinese?" We have been eating at the same Chinese restaurant–The Cottage on the corner of Amsterdam Avenue and 77th Street–on Sundays all of our life together. I know Harv likes to bet with Peter the owner on basketball games, so when we go over to the place to eat, they talk about what teams they like in the coming weeks.

On another tape, Suzanne speaks of honoring life by continuing to confront the obstacles placed before her.

I see how Harv is always fighting against what he feels are his neurotic tendencies, and I try to do the same. I struggle to stand apart from what I think is the view other people have of me. I must come up with a better definition of myself and what I think of as my essence. I just worry that I will reach out and fail. I'm always worrying about failing and feeling humiliated. Somewhere within my disability itself, I must find a message to tell me how to continue living with hope and inspiration. I must find some significance for myself. I can't leave this to Harv to do for me. He tries to fill me with imagination about my purpose on earth. I think he's afraid that I don't get it, but I do.

Saving Beauty

At moments, I wondered who Suzanne had become. She was no longer a therapist, no longer a woman with an intellectual or a sexual life. Increasingly, she remained at home, giving up even the pretext of being her old self. Suzanne's entire standing in society had been completely revised. Her relegation to a wheelchair put her in a different category of human beings–the disabled ones. Most of her time she spent alone, staring at the walls in our apartment, or facing our fifty-two-inch television screen, complete with surround sound. She was pulled back into herself by a sense of loss and inadequacy.

"The outside world is for those who have whole bodies – who can manage steps, subways, taxicabs, who don't need curb-cuts to maneuver the streets," she observed. I remember thinking about what it must have been like for people with disabilities before any urban planning considerations existed at all. The paralyzed patients living in the tenement slums on the docks in the early days of the century when electricity was a new commodity and blocks of ice were lugged to the tops of steps. Wheelchairs were the purview of the extremely wealthy. Without someone to push their chairs and get them up and down curbs, they were confined to their apartments. Suzanne had not been able to go anywhere alone for the past five years. She always needed help, either from our caregiver or myself.

I established a routine of working out at a local gym three days a week. I lifted weights to develop my upper body strength so I could carry Suzanne and transfer her from wheelchair to car seat, and from chairs to bed. I marveled at the strange twist of fate that we had been dealt. In the gymnasium my body could work perfectly, strengthening, acquiring greater strength and agility. It seemed unfair that I could blossom physically in the middle of life in contrast to her slow withering. I teased her that my new physique was the only good thing to have come out of this ordeal. She snapped back: "It's always all about you, isn't it?" The laughter was fast and real, she floated in a haze but she was still the woman who confronted me, who saw the boy within me and didn't hesitate to both celebrate and challenge me.

It was critical that I develop the physical strength to lift Suzanne if she fell. The first time Suzanne fell in my presence she became pale and silent, so frightened she couldn't respond to me. Her silence masked her terror that I wouldn't be able to get her up. I had so much trouble lifting her that I felt helpless and frustrated and out of control. I imagined dialing 911, calling the super or the doorman, lying on the floor with her, sharing in the helplessness and the odd feeling that yet a new milestone had happened without our expecting it. The moment when we couldn't function as a couple. The shame of having to turn things over to a new and stronger hands of paid strangers. That time I managed to control myself and finally raised her into a chair. But there were other times when she fell that I was defeated. Once I had to call for the superintendent to come and help me. I told Suzanne my shame for having to turn to the superintendent for help.

"Oh, Harv," she laughed. "This is bound to happen. Let's not make too big a deal of it. One of us is a klutz. The question is, which one?" When I didn't answer, she went on. "I've never been a klutz in my life, but I seem to remember you once referred to yourself that way."

"When?" I asked, not wanting to hear the answer.

"I hate to bring this up," she grinned. "But don't you remember telling me about the time when you were first opening your office and took off your shoes and got up on a Formica table in your socks to change an overhead bulb?"

"All right," I groaned. "Don't go on."

"Maybe you'd like to finish the story?" Suzanne suggested, her eyes alive with pleasure as she teased me.

"I slid off the table and broke a small bone in my thumb and had to wear a cast for three months. Does that make you happy?"

"It sure does," she giggled with girlish delight, sitting snugly in a chocolate brown chair. "Klutz!"

If disease talks about the changes in the body, illness relates to the fear and frustration of being inside a body that is going through so much turmoil. What was happening to Suzanne's body was also affecting her pleasures and desires. Medical questions could often be answered, specific symptoms could be alleviated even if temporarily by a pill, but the question of the meaning of her life was a vast blank that perplexed us both. She knew she could not continue her previous life as if nothing changed because everything was different.

If her dreams of the future had been altered then so were mine. If she couldn't envision herself traveling to distant parts of the world than I couldn't either. These previous fantasies had to be replaced, but our lives couldn't be redefined as a chronicle of sacrifice and stasis. We knew we had to lighten our trip together and seize upon whatever fun we could experience. Once she knocked over a cup of coffee all over the bed.

"You are really clumsy," my voice flared in a sudden jet of rage.

She looked up, her teeth bared like a tigress about to pounce, her lips curled back with indignation, spitting with contempt, "You know what? Sue me."

We both laughed, and I realized the terrible thing that just happened was trivial and insignificant.

But there were times when I lost my composure. To spare myself the feeling of helplessness, I sometimes laid the blame on her and accused her of being careless. At times I screamed at her. On one occasion, I actually pulled her hair to get her up from her armchair. Suzanne observed with a keen perception, I was at my meanest when I was most helpless. "Harv, I'm not going to take it anymore." Her manner was cool, with a blend of playfulness and a seriousness edge in her voice. She meant business. "I don't know whether to call a lawyer or a psychiatrist or just take more vitamins and throw something at you, sweetheart." She retained the confident spitfire of the woman who went to Easthampton and left me to wander around in Greece alone. When she grew irate, I promised her that I would never do such a thing again, and for the rest of our marriage, I kept that promise. Sometimes I yelled at her, but never again physically hurt her. Caregiver burnout has become a popular topic in the past decade. For a long time, I was in denial about my own burnout. Denial can be adaptive, but it can be the most maladaptive force in the human psyche. As Suzanne's caregiver, I needed to figure out how to take care of myself so I could keep pace in the relentless marathon.

Eventually we devised methods of picking her up off the floor whereby I would raise her onto a stool and from there onto a chair. But it was never easy, for Suzanne wasn't able to help at all. She experienced herself as a terrible burden to me at those times, but she would never say this in her determination to retain whatever scraps of dignity remained.

Speaking into the tape recorder, Suzanne reached for a poignant candor about her condition and her future, stripped naked of illusions.

> For so long I felt I had a clear direction in mind. I was traveling down a road that was resplendent with foliage and was in full charge of my journey. And then a fork appeared in the road. I veered off to the left and onto a path that was barren and dry and whose terrain I didn't recognize. Now I have no idea where I'm going, and I'm terribly frightened about what will happen to me. I need to talk to Harv about our future together. What will it look like? How will our days proceed? Will each one lead monotonously into the next as they do now? I hate the boredom and the routine, but don't have the strength to change it. My schedule throughout the weeks and months consists primarily of doctor visits and a few lunches with old friends.

> There will be no new friends unless I move out to New Jersey permanently. The women there seem more at ease with my disability, but even there, it will be they who have to visit me. I can't go to their condos because almost all of the entrances have steps.

Her honesty prompted me to reconsider my own life. I wasn't passionate about Freudian analysis anymore. I liked being the president of my analytic institute. I loved administration, political infighting, and a variety of causes. I had been compelled by Freud's theories of complexes, infantile sexuality, and neurosis. But I didn't find much in his work that was pragmatically helpful in coping with Suzanne. I needed a psychology of love, of soul, of the meaning of life as detached from a theory of sexuality. Meanwhile a specter was always with me – not the specter of Suzanne's pale withering body, but the specter of who I was, an older man, someone who had trouble lifting her, someone who would require the assistance of others, the shame of strangers, albeit well concerned ones, entering into what had been a private dyadic oasis. For me, this was the most difficult turning point in the story. Until then, the disability had been about her. Now my limitations were part of our dyad. Every caregiver comes to terms with his own limitations. One becomes a better caregiver when one accepts this.

Her tapes represent an ongoing self-analysis:

> I am still left with the question, "What are you going to do with yourself now?" I have no answer to that. At one point we thought I could run for vice president of the Freudian Society. Some of the members encouraged me to run. Harv and his brother, Don, who once had been president of the place, thought I would probably would win. But I knew deep inside

me that traveling to board meetings, walking up and down stairs, and all the energy the position would demand would have been too much for me. I gave up the idea and we never mentioned it again.

More and more I felt cheated by life, but didn't want to dwell on that. I hated feeling sorry for myself, feeling like a loser, having to depend on people to do things for me, and needing them in a way I had never needed anyone before. I hated feeling restricted in life and ashamed of my condition. Being pushed around in a wheelchair ...the whole thing made me sick. Yet what could I do to make it different? Should I pray to some divine source for the strength to surmount this disease? I am not religious, so doubt that would have helped. Sometimes I don't want to reach out anymore. I'm not sure I can. I'm not even sure that people would be interested in me if I did.

We discussed the soul, as we read Hillman's book together, and excerpts from Anna Karenina and fragments of poetry. We lay in bed holding hands, waiting for the pills to take effect and decrease her shaking.

On one of her tapes, Suzanne observed:

I have been struggling to understand what Harv is trying to tell me about making contact with my innate image. This language is new to me, but I am beginning to think it's the only language that can make sense of what I am going through. The soul is the part of you that's concerned with goodness, with courage, friendship, and loyalty. Character has more to do with the actions we take and the way we live our lives, with the things that bother us and what we do about them, with how we treat ourselves and others.

Suzanne came to believe: "Our purpose in life can be seen as our soul in action. I know my soul is wrapped up in this will to live and continue my journey through life. It's in the qualities that define my character. I think our psyches plot our fates but that character isn't necessarily destiny, for if we work at it hard enough, we can change our characters, we can become better people. I think of the Vedas and the notion that the soul percolates around each hair follicle with more intensity that ten raging suns put together. Damn this disease for taking away that energy, but bless it for making me realize that it's in me, that something in me will go on even after this body of mine shuts down forever." For Suzanne, locating her soul and sensing its existence within her made her feel loved in a way that connected her to the universe; each time she connected to her soul, she was reborn into a world of new possibilities. This is why I stress the idea of soul in this book. The concept of soul may seem murky, quasi-religious and mystical. And it is. But if we lose sight of it when we look at people with disabilities, we are in danger of seeing them as burdens on society, as nuisances or eyesores we would wish to hide. Notice the impatience many people exhibit while waiting for a bus ramp to be lowered and raised so a wheelchair passenger can board. I know Suzanne used to feel embarrassed about the time it took her to board a bus, but she came to believe it was her right to take her time and get on that bus any way she could. So firmly did she believe this that once when I told her not to be concerned with what anyone else on the bus was feeling, she snapped back: "What makes you think I'm concerned with anyone else's feelings?"

Disability brings out character. Character nourishes the imagination. It gives us a path to follow and a purpose to live out. As Suzanne said, "To have this spiritual existence, I need heroic forms to live up to, patterns of excellence so high that I could achieve them rarely, if ever, images of perfection so exquisite that seeing someone live up to them, produces a kind of 'Ah' reaction." Suzanne's soul called on her to persevere and to confront impossible odds as she fought for her life.

> I knew the MS had all the power. Still, I couldn't reconcile myself to defeat. A voice kept speaking to me. Was it my soul? You

can't give in. You will prevail. I have willed this for you from your beginning. I love you and am so proud of the way you are handling this struggle. You keep me believing in life.

This voice kept me believing and wondering too.

Chapter Seven

Try a Little Tenderness

Dona Munker, author of Daughter of Persia, starts off her article "Enchantment and Biographical Passion" by saying that a desire to write seriously about another's life is the result of an enchantment for one's subject. Writing passionately about the life of another person is a way of falling in love with that person and his or her story. I am driven by a need to tell her story as well as I can. It is the story of three lives: hers, mine, and what I see as a third life–the one we created together.

Stories are less about logic than they are about truth. They have the power to mend us when we feel defeated and to heal us when we are sick. They help us make sense of our lives. The holocaust continues to generate narratives, screenplays, and novels because it is a vast chasm in human behavior we are all seeking to come to grips with. Suzanne's struggle, in turn, gave definition and purpose to my own life and created that third life, the one we shared together. I am telling the story of these three lives not as a tale of disability and endurance, but as a story of healing through imagination and fantasy.

I believe that we come to understand the world in two different ways. One comes through logical proof or scientific reasoning. The other comes through concern with human wants, needs, and visions. To tell this story as a chronology of Suzanne's MS would be to attempt to achieve understanding primarily through dates and logic and facts. I would rather search for the narrative truth that emerges when we look at human needs and intentions, frustrations and fantasies.

I remember a vacation to Rome in the early years of our marriage. We walked up the Spanish Steps to the Keats museum, marveling as we read his correspondence that he had died at 26. We considered the portrait gallery of his friend Shelley, of his wife, and the tangle of lives that had ended in strange ways centuries earlier. There was a copy of Keats' letter written in his confident penmanship, even as he was dying of tuberculosis, to his family, proclaiming that it was a misnomer to call the world a 'vale of tears.' Keats' advice was to: "Call the world if you please 'the vale of Soul-making.' Then you will find out the use of the world…I say 'Soul-making', Soul as distinguished from an Intelligence. There may be intelligences or sparks of divinity in millions – but they are not Souls till they acquire identities, till each one is personally itself." Keats took for granted the immortality of human nature. His account of 'Soul-making' relates to the uses surrounding identity and creativity.

Suzanne had already been sick for a few years during that trip to Rome but she could walk up the winding steps of the museum without assistance. She was breathless but eager to discuss his ideas. Keats viewed romantic art as something that strives to achieve the union of the soul and its objects. In romantic love, lovers strive to unite their two souls and in the process, transformation takes place. The making of a poem is the poet's way of completing the process of love. In the world of the imagination the poet expresses the depths of his inner world and comes closer to the meaning of his soul. I am trying to understand what it means to make contact with another's defining image as it reflects their inner essence.

That afternoon back in our hotel overlooking the Tiber we made love with a peculiar violence, as if a fissure was opening up between us that only the heat of our bodies moving together could soothe, all the first fire of our passion returned to our bodies. When it was over Suzanne wept and my head was heavy like a stone against her breast until we started the ancient grinding of the mortar and pestle again. The heat of the afternoon. The buzzing of Italian cars in the Roman rush hour and the memories of the museum made us dizzy with happiness. Later we walked through the streets and ate gelato like children, licking fragoli and pistaccio off of our fingers. Throwing coins into fountains and fondling stray cats that greeted us like long lost friends.

Suzanne had a private life that remained forever secret, even from me. As open as she was about many things, she was reticent about her previous romances. She told me once about a previous lover she had lived with at the University of Maryland. As an analyst I've learned that intimacy doesn't mean telling each other everything. It's telling the other what's necessary for the contact between the two people to flow. In the most fulfilling marriage, there are stories that do not need be told. These belong to earlier parts of life. Perhaps they are no longer relevant, or are extremely relevant but belong to each person's inner world of erotic and romantic history. Psychoanalysis and most modern psychotherapies are based on excavating the past, but in the service of seeing how the past can help people behave in more constructive ways now – in the immanence of the present moment.

From the moment she came to New York, she surrounded herself with successful people. One of her friends worked in advertising, one was a prosperous Wall Street broker, another was a respected psychoanalyst. A close childhood friend was making a successful career change. They were all drawn to Suzanne's kinetic energy. It was largely this group that remained her friends to the end. They engaged with Suzanne at the most primal and passionate level of energy. As things progressed they were able to see that spark still burning within her –essential energy that was a part of her primordial essence.

My memories of Suzanne pop up out of order and bring back random thoughts of great times we had together. On our tenth wedding anniversary, I took her to hear Bobby Short, who was playing at the Café Carlyle. I made reservations for dinner in the hotel's dining room. We arrived early and as we were studying the wine list and wondering what to order, I happened to notice who was seated at the table next to ours. I nudged Suzanne and angled my head.

"Wow!" she whispered. "That's Bobby Short."

"Wait a moment." I took a small card propped on our table and walked over to him. "Bobby," I said, as if I had known him forever. "This is a special evening for us. Would you mind autographing this card?"

"What's the occasion?" he asked. When I told him it was our tenth anniversary, he laughed and casually slapped me on the back. "That's splendid. I'm honored that you chose to spend it with me." He took the card and wrote in a large expansive script: *Happy 10th. All the best, Bobby Short.*

Suzanne beamed with pride and nodded at Bobby Short to thank him. He nodded back and grinned. "Good luck, you two are love birds, I can always tell."

Suzanne and I traveled to exotic places, world class cities, and attended spectacular performances. Still, in retrospect, a nagging voice inside my head tells me that there could have been more, reconsiders opportunities that were missed, wonders why I didn't take her to hear so many other great artists while she as alive. I could have created so many other vivid memories for myself. Why didn't I? I am the one who lost out, for those memories will never live in my imagination to help heal my loss. And yet I know that no life is simple and no life can contain everything. Mortality brings all the threads of any given life to a point of closure that acknowledges that life is specific, limited, confined to a period in time. Picasso devoted his genius to painting, Proust to literature, and Freud to understanding the darkest recesses of the human mind. A rational part of me tells me that regrets are foolish. But the romantic in me believes that regrets can become as sacred as memory. The things that you haven't done can become a tremendous source of romance and excitement – the exquisite lure of the road not taken. As children, many of us wondered what life would be like if we were immortal and had all the time in the world to do whatever we wanted. The truth is that we narrow as we grow older. Suzanne's disease brought that issue into sharp focus as if she were aging in a time warp that had accelerated without warning. It is the nature of every life as the soul hurtles ahead towards destiny. As we age, fewer possibilities exist. No given life can encapsulate everything. It's a form of hubris to imagine that it could. But as we give up the hope that we will go everywhere and do everything we want, we are able to replace this loss with the depth of contact with another, an intense encounter with the intensity of the choices that we have made, and the humility of realizing that not everything is possible, all projects cannot be finished, and we may never say what we meant to say perfectly or completely. Regrets need not cause sadness, but rather can become a greater stimulation to claim more of what our experience on this earth has to offer us.

I have been practicing psychotherapy for almost thirty-five years. In the beginning I felt tremendous excitement about my career path. I had many patient hours and was quite successful. I believed profoundly in the capacity of psychotherapy to change human behavior not just individually, but at social and political levels. I read books by radical psychiatrists like Wilhelm Reich on the *Mass Psychology of Fascism* and thought seriously if there were less sexual repression could the Nazis have risen to power, or was aggression an innate aspect of our humanness, forged in our earliest experiences by feelings of deprivation in relation to the ultimate limitations of mothering and the breast. But in the end it wasn't theory that predominated in my life, but the desire to bring people together, to be a leader, to see an organization grow outside of the boundaries of individual offices with couches and secret confessions, slow insights gained over years. Eventually I became president of NPAP and have been serving on its board of directors for close to twenty years.

I was always interested in clinical work, but over the years I found it harder to immerse myself in the theoretical aspects of the field – the countless articles in journals and scientific presentations. I look at my colleagues and wonder if they still maintain a deep interest in psychoanalysis? Do they live it and breathe it, as I once did? I discussed this with Suzanne, and she told me that she had always thought I needed interests outside of the range of psychoanalysis. She noticed that what I read and what excited me were the realms of literature and politics. Being close to issues of life and death inspired a hunger for more from the world. I needed Shakespeare and Tolstoy more than Freud. I wanted to understand the jealousy of Iago, the determination of Henry V, the transcendence of Levin, more than I wanted to comprehend the Wolf Man. I hungered for art and culture that spoke of the precious tapestry of life and suffering.

Being close to Suzanne and sharing in her head-on confrontation with life and death gave me less tolerance for procrastination and regret. As she changed, I changed along with her. Perhaps this is the blessing of the disease. It makes us take a good honest look at what we want and inspires us to act on our desires in the present moment.

It was Suzanne's destiny to contract MS. What is mine? I often wondered. Before I met Suzanne, I dated Donna, a wonderful woman who had two children close to my daughter's age. Shortly after we broke up, Donna met a man who moved in with her. Sometimes I had second thoughts about breaking up with Donna. She was a tantalizing regret, an example of the road not taken. What would it have been like if…?

Five years ago, I ran into Donna again and we spent some time catching up. When we parted, I wondered if I had made a mistake in not marrying her. Had I done so, I would have been spared the burden of MS and my life would have been so much easier. Then I thought about Suzanne's life and what it would have been like if she had not married me or had never married at all. What if she had married someone who didn't stay with her once she fell ill? Or knowing her conviction and strength, I believe if I had passed out of her life at that party years ago, her vibrant charm would have attracted someone else, equally good, a different soul mate who would have seen her through to the end. Such thoughts unleash a deep sensation of loss within me, and yet I can't avoid picking at them like a scab, opening the wound over again, seeing the blood and the plasticity of flesh reforming. Proof that even death is not immutable. "No," I sing the old Gus Kahn song to myself. "It had to be you."

I thought of a spring day when I had pushed Suzanne's wheelchair to that spot she loved in Riverside Park where she could watch the dogs racing up and down the dog-run. Her eyes were shining as they followed the dogs at play. The radiance of her spirit at that moment made me take her hand and tell her that it was good to see her looking so happy. The water on the river glimmered with white light and the air was filled with the subtle scent of a wysteria pushing into bloom.

A dog approached Suzanne's beckoning hand, and she ran

her hands slowly down his back, through the drool of his mouth as he sat at the feet of her wheel chair. Then he rushed off to join the others in the whirling dervish of ecstasy.

Suzanne pulled my hand towards her face. She was crying. "Don't worry Harv. I'm just so happy."

Blood rushed through the capillaries of my chest and contentment pulsed in the soft motor of my heart. "Remember how you used to say, it's all about me? Well, it's all about us now, no matter what."

Suzanne's illness made me look at the city in new ways. And what I noticed was that even buildings you would expect to have provisions for people with disabilities often didn't. I made it a rule not to take Suzanne anywhere without first checking out the building's accessibility. Once, however, we were invited to a wedding at The Ethical Culture Society, some twelve blocks from our home, and I neglected my rule. I dressed Suzanne, applied makeup to her face, and got her into her wheelchair. I pushed her the twelve blocks and when we arrived in front of the building, I was shocked to find six steps going up to the lobby and another six going down to the ballroom. It should have been so simple. An evening of entertainment in our neighborhood. Without warning, an impossible barrier was staring at us, ruining our plans. Embarrassment flooded me. How had I not foreseen something so simple?

Suzanne considered the steps, and then looked at me. "What do you want to do?" she asked.

I considered turning around and going home in despair. Then two strong building workers came over, lifted Suzanne up the front steps, took her down to the ballroom and promised to come back for her when the reception was over.

"I'm so sorry about putting you through all that lifting and carrying," I told her.

"Oh, Harv," she replied. "It's not that bad. Let's just have a good time."

I still feel that institutions need to be more sensitive to the needs of people with disabilities. I write letters and join campaigns. I see gradual changes in the city. Ubiquitous curb cuts, wheelchair accessible bathrooms on the floors of orchestras and theaters, taxis and buses equipped with hydraulic lifts for wheelchairs. In the gradual instant of evolution transformation is possible. I think of a time one hundred years after my death and perhaps this disease will no longer exist at all.

I didn't always press Suzanne to tell me her darkest fears. I sometimes shied away from knowing too much of what she was feeling, believing there wasn't much I could do. I had developed enough powers of self-analysis through therapy to understand that in giving her the tape-recorder I was giving her a positive tool to find her voice, but was also deflecting her words away from me. I attempted to find a barrier with which I could protect myself, with which I could define my life as being separate from hers, unattached to the demands of this illness. At times I became impatient with Suzanne. Too often I answered her calls for assistance with, "Can't it wait?" or "Just a moment." I knew I should have been more considerate. I understood how much her authority had diminished over the course of her illness and how inadequate this made her feel. But I couldn't stop myself from wanting to create a subtle degree of distance. If Suzanne were trapped in a pool with deadly vines encircling her, I was willing to visit that pool but remained frightened of getting too close to the water. I grew impatient with her for not striving harder to find new meaning in her life after she was forced to give up her career. Ultimately, nothing could substitute for the life's purpose she had enjoyed as a psychotherapist. I wanted to provide this purpose for her and knew I couldn't. When I spoke to her about the need to make an extra effort to find meaning in her life, I could hear the artificiality in my voice and my words sounded as if they had been taken from some banal self-help guide.

As I watched Suzanne create a private world for herself, I often thought, "Let her keep it to herself. Do I need to get involved ?" My friends and family were concerned at times. "Harv, you're amazing at being supportive. But you've also got to consider yourself. What's happening to you, you need to get out more."

I learned a technique that helped tremendously. The more I focused on my own life and feeling resourceful about myself, the more I was able to be receptive to the continuous onslaught of Suzanne's disease. As a caregiver, you can visit the black despair of your loved one, but if you sink into it, both of you will be lost. I did my best to respond to her sense of inadequacy, her feelings of uselessness. Yet I was happy she didn't express these feelings too often. She maintained a composure that both impressed and shamed me. I knew that, were the situation reversed, I would not have handled it as well. Love, disease and death are the great playgrounds and obstacles of life. Each person is on his own path. Even the deepest loves have limits, places they cannot go. While Suzanne's story and mine intertwined, they were also different. I needed to set the limits that I did. If battling a chronic debilitating illness is a marathon, pacing is everything.

In 1985, some months after Suzanne was diagnosed with MS, we went to Spain. After three days in Madrid, we rented a car and drove north into the Basque country. Our first stop was the coast town of San Sebastian. Suzanne had expected that we would continue on to the south of France. I had given her a vague idea of our itinerary but told her to expect some surprises. One was Lourdes.

"Why Lourdes?" Suzanne asked. "We're not even Catholic."

"We're going to make a pilgrimage."

"A what?"

"You heard me, and you don't have to be Catholic to have hope."

We drove through the Pyrenees into Lourdes and found a room in a hotel not far from the Cathedral of Bernadette. We walked through the village and bought a number of trinkets and medals commemorating Saint Bernadette, which I keep in a small wooden box in my bureau to this day. That evening we watched an inspiring procession winding slowly through the village and across its bridge, the people holding lighted candles and singing the Ave Maria. Did I expect a miracle? We met many who did – people with cancer and multiple sclerosis, muscular dystrophy and Parkinson's disease, the blind and the paraplegic. We talked with a man whose wife's legs had been crushed in an automobile accident. He explained that he was going to stay several extra days in hope that his wife would leave the place in better condition than she had arrived.

I told Suzanne I didn't know if anything would come of this, but maybe if we believed in it would we stood a better chance.

"Now I know why you were reading *The Song of Bernadette*," she laughed.

And then she became serious. "But, Harv, I don't believe in miracles."

"At least try to believe in their possibility," I countered. "What do we have to lose?" I realized that this leap of faith was harder for the sick than the healthy. "Maybe you are right. Nothing may come of this, but nothing will happen if we don't try to believe. That's for sure."

Science was a palimpsest of ideas and theories that took shape and generated excitement and then receded – offering no cure for MS. Sometimes supernatural events made as much sense to us, if not more.

Harvey A. Kaplan

The next day we walked along a ridge to the shrine in the grotto where Bernadette had seen the vision of the Virgin Mary. Outside the grotto, glistening geysers of water erupted from the ground. There were rumors of their miraculous healing powers. Suzanne and I knelt and drank the waters. Later in the day we visited the majestic cathedral erected for Bernadette. To have made this pilgrimage, I must, on some level, have believed that miracles were possible if one placed one's hopes in the hands of a higher power. This may sound odd coming from a Jew, but to me Christianity has never been a particularly foreign religion. Suzanne was not Catholic, or remotely interested in the doctrines of Christianity. For some reason, the actual rules of a religion never mattered to me. I believe there is a power within us that has the capability to reach a higher level, a deeper connection to our spirit. I'm moved by hands clasped in prayer, invoking contact with the divine, the ethereal, the forces that move through the universe that we cannot understand.

Throughout Suzanne's illness, I believed she would outlive me. The idea frightened me, for I wondered who would take care of her and how she would get on after I was gone. One Saturday while I was taking my usual bike ride through the hills near our place in New Jersey, I found I couldn't make it up one not terribly steep hill, so I turned around and went back to the condo. "That was a quick ride," Suzanne said. I didn't want to frighten her, so I made up some story about cramps in my legs. Then it dawned on me that I had also been feeling exhausted days earlier on the treadmill. I made an appointment to see my physician. After conducting the requisite tests, he told me that I was having a heart attack. I froze. Was this the way I would finally leave Suzanne? He informed me that he was admitting me to the hospital immediately. I told him that was impossible.

"Why?" he demanded.

Saving Beauty

"It's Friday," I replied. "I can't go without knowing that someone will take care of Suzanne for the weekend."

"Weekend?" he cried. "We're talking about weeks."

This startling news did not fit in my love map. I was not prepared to be the sick one. And above all, I didn't want to worry her. Even if I were to die from a sudden massive myocardial infraction, this seemed merciful compared to the years of disability Suzanne had endured.

I went home, knowing I had to tell Suzanne something, but not wanting to mention the words heart attack. "The doctor thinks I need to have my heart monitored," I informed her as calmly as I could. "So he's making arrangements to get me into Lenox Hill today." I turned to Lenore, our Monday-to-Friday caregiver, and asked her to stay with Suzanne for however long I was in the hospital.

About noon on that Friday, I checked in at the emergency room and submitted to another battery of tests. Finally, an actual doctor appeared.

"We don't think it's a heart attack," he reassured me. "It's some kind of fibrillation problem, but we have to wait for the cardiologist for confirmation on that."

I got to my room about two A.M., flooded with relief.

Later that morning, the cardiologist came in with a broad grin on his face. "How are you doing?"

"I'd be doing a lot better, if you told me I wasn't having a heart attack."

"Your EKG would indicate that, but what you're having is an atrial flutter. There is an easy procedure to reverse the process. All we do is insert a wire and burn the sinus node, and that will give you a normal heartbeat. Feeling better?"

Relieved, I called Suzanne and told her the news. Later that day as I was lying in bed, she came scooting into my room with Lenore trailing behind.

"Hey, you didn't have to come," I said, immensely grateful that she had.

"Of course I had to come. You're my husband."

I smiled at her through tears, "And here we thought you were the sick one."

She had researched atrial flutter on the Internet. "It's the most minor of heart problems," she announced, every inch the doctor's daughter. "Fibrillation would be more serious. You would have to be on a blood thinner for the rest of your life. You're lucky that wasn't it."

The afternoon sun glinted through the hospital windows, burning off the smell of disinfectants and disease. Her hand was in mine, and her eyes were lively, as she told me about the various world events that I had missed. She stroked me back into the cozy consistency of our love.

Prior to meeting Suzanne I had always been able to reach deep into myself and find reservoirs of resilience when I most needed them. I had failed out of one graduate school, but then rebounded, applied to, and was accepted by another completing a doctorate in a demanding and competitive environment. But these were conscious, reality-oriented issues. Suzanne's illness took me to places of emotional and psychological strength I never knew I possessed. I look back and count the gifts of the illness. I compare the young man I was to the man I am now in my seventies. I consider how I've overcome my shortcomings. I conquered my temper and impatience. I became a better person for having known Suzanne. I wrestled with a complex situation, and I had the temerity not to run away from it. But I was still human. I resented her illness at times. I resented the limitations it put on our lives, the passion it took out of it. I resented her for having it and then succumbed to guilt about my resentment. A friend who once listened patiently to all my complaints asked, "If you were the one with MS, would she even think of leaving you?" I smiled. I knew she wouldn't, no more than I would ever leave her. In sickness and in health. For better and for worse. Over years we grew into those words.

In 1988, Suzanne was diagnosed with breast cancer. She was visibly shaken, yet incredibly brave. The first thing she asked the doctor was, "What are my options?" She was told she couldn't have chemotherapy because it would exacerbate the MS. A bilateral mastectomy was indicated, and quickly. She lowered her head to hide her tears. Her breasts were emblematic of youth and passion. I recalled photos of Suzanne, taken in her early twenties, on the powdery white sand of the Côte d'Azur. She was wearing a bikini. Her body was exquisite, her breasts stunning. And she would lose them – on top of everything else. I wondered how much any one person could stand.

Shortly before the operation, Suzanne took my hand as we lay in the darkness.

"I'm not sure I can go through with this operation. How can I give up my breasts?" Her voice was a faint wisp of smoke, barely audible in the room.

"Do you have any idea of how many women die of breast cancer every year?" I asked her. "I follow the obits in the Times, and hardly a day goes by without a notice about a woman who died from breast cancer. I know it's a terrible blow. I know how proud you've always been of your breasts, but what's important is that you'll live."

Suzanne survived the breast surgery and had silicone implants inserted. They were successful at a cosmetic level, but after a few years, the chronic burning pain along the tracks of scar tissue became intolerable, and she had the implants removed. The surgeons could have reconstructed her breasts after the operation, but her MS contraindicated the procedure, so they decided against it. In the end, the MS took precedence over everything else.

Harvey A. Kaplan

In *Cherishment: A Psychology of the Heart*, Elisabeth Young-Bruehl and Faith Bethelard trace the idea of cherishment to the writings of the Japanese psychoanalyst Takeo Doi. In Japanese, the common verb, amaeru, means "to wish or to expect to be loved." This word has no counterpart in English. Amae is the noun derived from the verb, meaning the silent expectation of being. Being cherished is accomplished, not spoken. Responding to an adult's desire to be cherished entails picking up on silent cues. You have to "get it," sense it, feel it empathically. It's more than love for the other. It's an intuitive understanding of dependency and need to be loved. A mother knows what her own child needs because she remembers when she herself was a child. By identifying with her former self, she becomes exquisitely attuned to her child's needs. As adult caregivers, we also know what the person with a disability needs by identifying with our childhood selves.

As Suzanne's illness worsened, my love for her became more focused on caring and loyalty, and endurance more than on passion, and adventure. Had it not, I would not have been able to bear the grief of her disability or the abandonment of so many dreams for our future. It is my clinical opinion that empathy can change people as much and perhaps more than insight into childhood dynamics. As I look back on the life we shared, empathy was the glue that held us together. We opened our hearts to each other – learning how to hold each other and how to let go. Empathy sustains me now, as I want to believe – in the face of widespread terrorism and disease – that we are part of a complex mosaic of shifting truths moving ever closer towards the light.

Chapter Eight

You Make Me Feel So Young

Love is the most omnipotent word in our language. In its name, illnesses have been cured and hopes lifted. According to Freud, the patient's love for the analyst is the curative factor in psychoanalysis.

Once Suzanne's MS was in full swing, my love for her underwent a profound transformation, which allowed our relationship to survive as Suzanne changed both physically and mentally. I changed, too. Awards, professional recognition and unreturned phone calls all ceased to matter in the wake of Suzanne's struggle. I became her nurturer and friend – the trainer in her corner who kept her motivated and spurred her on through moments of crushing defeat. I was like the person who "spots" a weightlifter – standing behind the one lying on the bench, pressing weights. By placing his hands on the barbell to take some of the weight, the spotter offers support and allows the weightlifter to take more risks.

"I can't do this alone," Suzanne often remarked. I kept reminding her that she was not alone. She had me, as well as many close friends who were passionately involved in her life. The shark had singled her out. While we surrounded her – offering a helping hand from our position of safety – we could not imagine the pain of teeth tearing into her flesh. She was alone with her incontinence, the insidious paralysis, the struggle to find a half an hour when she could be certain of the time and place before the flickering neurons failed leaving her in a confused fog again. It was she who faced a lonely, debilitating death. As Shakespeare says in Henry V, the king is responsible for the kingdom, but everyman's soul is his own. When she was discouraged, sometimes my words reached her, and I could feel the bridge opening up between us again, as it did that first night at the party. But now she was no longer lively and vivacious. Her eyes burned with a liquid emotion, as she lay in bed, and I encouraged her: "You have a soul that wants to be loved, to be heard and seen. Your soul wants you to live."

One evening we were driving back to the city after visiting her parents in Baltimore. As the gray contour of the Manhattan skyline emerged in the distance, her tone grew serious, and I could sense that she had come to a decision.

"I need someone with me during the day while you're at the office. I'm finding it harder and harder to dress myself, to make meals, and even to go out alone. I didn't bring this up before because I thought you wouldn't like the idea, but I can't put it off any longer. I'm worried that I might fall, maybe break my ankle again." She had broken her ankle while we were visiting a friend in the Berkshires. I had rushed her to the hospital, where she had steel plates inserted. She spent the rest of the summer in our condo in New Jersey, never leaving the house, and when we got back to the city, she sat and slept in a reclining chair in the living room for over a month. I didn't want either of us to have to endure this again.

"I'll take care of it," I assured her.

"When?" she asked. Her tone wasn't an accusing one but there was a tension in it, reminding me of my plans that never were completed, ideas that never materialized. Her voice was serious business – warning me that this time there could be no fumbling, no delay.

"As soon as we get back," I promised. "I'll call Gary and find out what agency he used." Gary was a friend who had hired a caregiver for his mother and was pleased with the person his agency found for them.

"Okay."

When I looked at her, I saw her wide, pleading eyes. "Harvey, please, just do it soon. You don't know what it's like being alone in the house and being afraid about what could happen."

"Don't worry," I told her. I tried to see the world from her point of view – the empty uncertainty of the day stretching before her. Not knowing if she would move or fall or fracture a bone; whether she would be able to get to a telephone. She wore an emergency alert device around her neck, that was linked to an ambulance service. As time progressed she activated that button several times. But Suzanne was still terrified of her own helplessness. "Harvey, you've got to understand this. Time stands still when you're laying on the floor in pain, wondering if help will arrive."

I looked into her eyes and promised. "We'll get the best person for you we can. She'll be around a lot."

The first woman the agency sent us was a kinetic redhead without a green card whose hyperactivity made us nervous. Lenore, the next candidate in line, had emigrated from Trinidad where she had been an elementary school teacher. Her small, contained frame exuded a quiet maternal authority. In her presence one experienced stillness, the feeling of walking from a hot crowded street into the cooler air of a temple. Lenore had taught home economics, loved to cook, read the papers every day, was interested in current events and politics, and wrestled with bringing up six children. We hired her on the spot.

Almost immediately, Lenore and Suzanne became the best of friends. They went to movies and watched the television news together. They discussed current events and did the shopping and cooking together. They seemed more like sisters than caregiver and client. Eventually they started going to the theatre together and visiting Suzanne's friends. Lenore gave Suzanne an anchor. Her mood lifted, and her old insouciance returned.

"Thank you, Harv," she whispered as I bent down and stroked her, a current of happiness pulsing between us. "Thank you for Lenore."

Lenore stayed with us for six years before deciding to return to her husband and five grown children in Trinidad. Her loss was hard on Suzanne, who by that time could no longer stand or move herself to and from her wheelchair. Now she required live-in help. We needed someone who had a personality compatible with Suzanne's and was also strong enough to lift her. After a short time, we found Mana, a former physician from Kiev.

By this time we had decided that Suzanne would be happier and more comfortable living in the country full-time. Mana had a driver's license, so she could do the shopping in town and pick me up at the station when I came out for the weekends. And like Lenore, she was smart, well read, took part in conversations, and got on well with Suzanne. Suzanne's relief was palpable. The psychological and social benefits she derived from the arrangement were even more important to her than the physical fact of having someone to assist her with things she could no longer do by herself. Again, sisterly love and ebullient camaraderie blossomed between them, and I was aware of an inexplicable happiness that was different from anything I had ever known. As I look back on those times, I don't remember the sickness as much as the laughter, the food, the conversations, and the sense of rich, textured life that would last as long as it could.

We knew that the treatments Suzanne was receiving were more palliative in nature than curative. And often the drugs caused her more discomfort than relief. For quite some time, she had been taking Avonex (a derivative of interferon) once a week. After each dose the drug produced a low-grade fever, which sent her to bed for two days. It took us years to realize that the drug wasn't improving her functioning in any way. In fact, its side effects were making her feel worse. When Suzanne stopped taking it, she immediately improved. It was hard to balance our longing for a medication that could slow down the disease – offering us another five or ten years of life together – with the stark reality that most of the treatments had uncertain benefits and horrendous side effects.

Only a few years after Suzanne's death, the armamentarium of medications is changing radically. A host of new agents are on the market with promising results, -- Avonex, Btaseron, Cpaxone or Rebif. If Suzanne would have taken one of these medications earlier on in the course of her illness the story might have had a radically different outcome. She might be here with me now. My prayer for the world is that in my lifetime there are significant advances in myelin repair which will restore function in damaged myelin. That there are fewer paralyzed people parading towards the waters of Lourdes and fewer victims of immobilizing illness trapped in isolation in apartments where no one visits. Suzanne might have regained her functioning under these conditions. It is hard to conceive of the fact that autoimmune diseases, such as multiple sclerosis afflict 24.5 million Americans. Autoimmune diseases are one of the top 10 leading causes of death among children and women under 65. Yet, less than 6 percent of Americans surveyed in a recent Roper poll understood what the definition of an autoimmune disease. Perhaps when we can all confront the discomfort in thought that arises when we contemplate disease and death we can push forwards as a global community to insist that science realize its possibilities to cure.

Barbara Webster remarks:

Hope is a necessary component of living with the disease, as it is a necessary part of life. But hope is possible only after full acceptance of present reality and potential consequences. ... For me, hope could only come into play after acceptance.

Acceptance came to us in stages. Weeks of denial alternated with weeks of allowing the physical realities to teach us this lesson. In the beginning, I thought that if Suzanne couldn't do something, it was because she wasn't trying hard enough. Surely, she could walk better if she tried. Certainly if she just worked harder, pushed harder, there must be some way of keeping the symptoms at bay. In the first stages I didn't go out of my way to help her do things like get in or out of the front seat of our car. I thought it would be better for her to try to function on her own. Even toward the end a fragment of my denial persisted. At times I continued to think that she probably could feed herself without help if she would put more effort into it. I see now that I was blaming the victim because I didn't want to face what was happening to her.

After many years, it became obvious that no cure for MS was forthcoming, and even if it were, Suzanne would never recover her former functioning. I would ask her what she was still able to hope for, and she told me that she found gratification in the world, music, flowers, friends and "the simple drama of life."

Suzanne taught me the meaning of "will to live." She possessed a tremendous desire to go on living. Disability diminishes our activity in life, but not necessarily our enjoyment. She was often able to live in what Frank calls the "Quest Narrative" – sensing that she has something to tell, something to pass on, how the illness impacts our journey.

Saving Beauty

At times, what was held out as hope often became an empty trial balloon. There were well meaning pseudo-scientists offering esoteric cures, the venom of bee stings, diets of coconut milk and raw eggs. And then there were the charlatans, the greedy, thieves trying to suck blood out of misfortune. One weekend on the ride up to Montague, I took along a copy of the New York magazine of March 18, 1991. There was a cover story by Tony Schwartz about a cardiovascular surgeon Dr. Irving I. Dardik. There was a photo of a lithe woman with frizzy blonde hair jumping on a trampoline, her teeth glinting in a smile of ecstasy. The headline read: "MAKING WAVES…CAN DR. IRV DARDIK'S RADICAL EXERCISE THERAPY REALLY WORK MIRACLES?" His treatment promised a complete remission of MS or your money would be refunded. I talked to Suzanne after reading this story. I told her that he had an office in Hackettstown which is not that far from us in New Jersey.

His theory had to do with regulating the heart rate to balance the immune system and thereby cure chronic autoimmune illnesses like MS. The article contained the anecdotal success stories of some six patients, some who were able to walk again and got over their chronic fatigue.

"Well, what do think? she asked me, raising a skeptical eyebrow.

I shook my head and paused. "I wish I could believe this, there is such great hope in it and yet it sounds contrived. What the hell does physical exercise have to do with struggling with the autoimmune system? And why should New York Magazine play this up so much. I think the best we can do is follow the story wherever it goes and then we will see."

We never pursued Dr. Dardik or any of the other unconventional therapies, and his name drifted out of mind. Several years later, I noticed a small piece in the New York Times about Dr. Dardik who was being sued for taking a MS patient's money and then deceiving her with his bogus treatment. After bilking her for thousands of dollar, he refused to answer her telephone calls. "Wow, that son of a bitch!" I thought as I leafed through the article. A murderous rage smoldered within me, wondering how many other people he had seduced and abandoned with his empty promises. It was a perverse trick to hold out hope when there was only illusion. He had a fashioned a clever but insidious game with a high profit margin. This unfortunate woman had spent several hundred thousand dollars, seduced into the false hope that she would recover.

A few years later, in the midst of a difficult weekend when Suzanne was too weak to lift her head to dictate into the tape recorder, I went down to the bookstore and browsed through titles on multiple sclerosis, hoping to find an anodyne. I bought "Legwork," a book by Ellen Burstein McFarlane. The sincerity of her gaze, captured in a black and white photograph on the back of the book, reassured me. Only as we read the book together did we realize that this was the same woman who had been duped by Dr. Dardik. Surrounding any illness lurks the possibility of other kinds of sickness – greed, charlatans, manipulation of hope, and gross dishonesty. Ellen held out for his bogus cure and now her condition was quickly deteriorating. In eight years she degenerated from her initial diagnosis to that of a triplegic who is confined to a wheelchair and needed full-time care. Incidentally, she saw many of the same doctors as Suzanne. She had a loving family and she had a fraternal twin sister, Patricia who never got the disease and who helped her write the book. I was impressed by her lack of bitterness, the betrayal did not cause her to lose hope. Her words unfolded a compassionate journey that provided inspiration on the gray days when despair seeped into our bones.

I remember as an undergraduate, getting drunk with my friends and laughing in our seminar on Saint Augustine. Save me god, save me but just not yet! And we'd look around at women in the bar or dance hall, wondering who we could score with, which pair of provocative eyes and lustrous hair might belong to the woman who would sculpt us into a future or leave us bruised and heartsick. We were young and embroiled in the world of the hot desiring machine of the body, not yet aware of the existence of something beyond the throbbing pressure of the flesh.

Suzanne understood this intuitively. She explored this on one tape:

> I don't think I have to deny what I am struggling with in order to nourish my soul and feel the good things I feel about myself. I am not deluding myself. I am telling myself that my body is not all there is. My struggle now is to give as much nourishment as I can to my soul.

My friends were no longer young undergraduates, wild and impatient, with eyes greedy for pleasure, hunting around for the future. Like me, they were middle-aged men, preoccupied with college tuitions and divorces and wondering if they would be downsized from their companies. A handful would take me aside, in some reversal of the feminist notion of woman as imprisoned helpmate, and ask me if I were imprisoned. If I needed a life of my own. If I should get out more. "You can't just let yourself become a slave to all of this. It's Suzanne's illness, not yours," one of my friends offered in consolation, gently slapping me on the back in the Oak Room. He had the burnished genteel tweeds of a prep school adolescence in Connecticut boarding schools. His smiling face was well intentioned, floating over a brandy snifter. "You gotta live a little, give a little. Don't you get it Harv?" We were both slightly buzzed from the liquor.

In nine out of ten pictures I see myself grinning, enduring the good natured frat boy and feeling a bit morally superior. But in the tenth picture I see his face naked and vulnerable, no longer alcoholic and effusive, but pleading with me to go on with my life. But that night I couldn't see that picture. "Trust me," I told him with an air of condescension, patting him back harder than I wanted to, "I'm in touch with reality. It's you who don't get it."

One of Freud's earliest and most important discoveries was the Oedipus Complex. The male child's love for his mother and envy of his father serves as a template for later triads. Jealousy, fear, and fantasy are often played out in triangular patterns. Even in the psychotherapist's office, three people are present: the therapist, the client, and the person the client is talking about – the observed self. This might be a younger self or an imagined self. In some ways the disease presented a new triangle, me and Suzanne and this rival of a disease – a mythic monstrous male energy that was taking her away from me, ravaging her, motivating me all the more to conquer and emerge victorious.

From my point of view, I had myself to consider; an ordinary man, at times elevated in my own fantasy life to the level of the heroic. At times the aching limitations of my own mortality, my own ebbing strength and patience, drove me to seek out time away from Suzanne -- a night with the boys, a mafia film I knew she wouldn't like, a way of escaping. Then there was the actual reality of what was involved in living with Suzanne's illness, wrestling with the disease and the mundane aspects of life – lists of medications and schedules for cleaning women to work on the condo and endless dates with her various doctors circled in colored ink in her calendar until her handwriting deteriorated too far for her to keep track of her appointments. There was the heroic, idealized Suzanne, the beauty queen who would go the final round with a deadly opponent and who excluded me from the battle, not out of deliberation, but out of necessity. I was in her corner, but I needed to see Suzanne in an idealized form, to keep sight of the vibrant personality that existed beyond her ravaged body. For me, her struggle personified her spirit. That's why I couldn't allow her to succumb to the feeling that illness was too overwhelming. This would have doomed our relationship.

Throughout her illness I struggled to tolerate uncertainty, frustration, and fear. But I knew I could not endure the loss of hope or the faith that love would provide the impetus to keep the relationship alive. Suzanne was not terminally ill until she contracted that infection in the hospital. Had she been able to overcome the infection, she might have lived for many more years and even outlived me, as I always assumed she would.

Much as I resented Suzanne's illness, it drew me closer to her and brought out a side of me that had never been called upon before. Softness, quiet, solitude, domestic ritual all became sacred in a way I never could have imagined when I was younger. I considered other people's lives with less judgment. I examined their childhood vulnerabilities, their potential brilliance, and their visions of what would be most important to them as they faced their own deaths. The most terrible hardships demand the bravest efforts and can bring forth a kind of love that you never knew you possessed. In a sense, MS sustained me. I knew it was here to stay and forgot what my life could be without it. Concealed in the illness itself was a secret kind of love waiting to be brought forth.

Over time, Suzanne became increasingly physically unattractive to me, having gained inordinate amounts of weight due to the prednisone she was taking, and having lost all muscle tone in her body because she was unable to exercise. I would gaze into her face, trying to find the glimmering of light emerging from her eyes, congealing now in mountains of flesh cascading over her once supple physique. She wanted me to be more amorous toward her, and because I wanted her to feel appreciated and desired, I attempted to relocate the passion that previously had filled our relationship. Yet I always knew I was doing it for her and not for me. I couldn't discuss this with her, knowing how cruel it would be to say I love you but not sexually anymore.

She confided to her tape recorder:

Harv never comes on to me anymore. He has lost interest in me as a sexual partner, and I'm embarrassed to bring this up to him. It's probably better not to, for if he's no longer attracted to me, there's nothing I can do about it. But my worst fear is that I am depriving him of a chance for basic human fulfillment. I keep him back from living a fuller life. I see the sacrifices he makes for me, but I would rather not think about them because it leaves me feeling so down.

While our sexual passion declined, our shared passion for music – Sinatra for me, opera for Suzanne – continued to play a vital role in our relationship. One night, shortly after we moved in together, I waited outside our building for Suzanne to come home after her last class at The Freudian Society.

When she saw me standing there on the street, her brow furrowed with concern. "Is there a problem?"

"No problem. I just want to show you something. They're shooting a movie on the next block."

Suzanne, knowing my popular heroes better than anyone, replied, "If you were willing to take the time to stand here on the street and wait for me, it can only be Frank Sinatra."

She was right. It was the winter of 1979 and they were filming *The First Deadly Sin* on West 80th Street. We walked to the corner and saw Sinatra ambling toward his trailer. A woman ran up to him and asked for his autograph. Sinatra obliged. I patted my jacket and coat pockets for a pen or pencil, but couldn't find one. Suzanne didn't have one either.

"How can you not have a pen when you were just taking notes in class?" I snapped at her.

"I had to borrow one," she explained.

We went home, disappointed and empty-handed.

Three years later, Suzanne threw a party for my fiftieth birthday. After the cake and champagne, Suzanne handed me her gift. It was the size of a coffee-table book and was wrapped in shiny, green paper. I thought it might be a photograph of the two of us together. But it was a signed photograph: To Harvey. Happy Birthday, Frank Sinatra.

"I knew you'd love it. And I hope it makes up for my not having a pen that evening."

Suzanne's gift was an expanded form of sexuality. She had reached inside me and gently stroked a side I held most dear. I started listening to Sinatra at the age of seven and have never stopped. By giving me this gift as I turned fifty, Suzanne not only made me feel young, but also honored a part of my life that predated our relationship and didn't directly include her. Perhaps it was her way of honoring my soul, realizing that it was different than hers, and celebrating it. In a New Yorker interview, the acclaimed conductor, composer, and pianist Andre Previn noted that we hold onto to the music of our adolescence all through our lives. The music we listened to as teenagers coincided with a burgeoning sexuality, the rebellion of a generation, the construction of a social self distinct from the family. Suzanne celebrated my entire life – the wildness of my boyhood in the Bronx, my years in the army, and the years that would come after she was gone.

I remember telling Suzanne a story of another popular singer I had worked with. Earlier in life, I had learned a lesson about living in the present. In 1952 I was still in college, I worked part-time as an usher in what was then the Fine Arts movie theatre on 58th Street and Lexington Avenue. I ushered with a guy who was about seventeen and called himself Bobby Walden. We worked together for close to a year, and for most of that year we saw the same French movie over and over. It was *Beauties of the Night*, starring Gerard Phillipe. After all that repetition, it's the score that I remember more than the plot. Bobby

Harvey A. Kaplan

Walden took to calling me "Kap." When, years later, I told Suzanne this story, I reminded her that no one other than herself and a few boys I had grown up with had ever called me Kap. Walden seemed fond of the name and we got along well. At the time he was performing regularly at small Westside bars at the time and always invited me to come and listen to him sing. Even at seventeen, he was so ambitious and knew what he wanted out of life.

"You gotta reach for the moon in this world, Kap," he used to say. "Nothing is going to stop me, you'll see."

One day in 1963, I did see. At that time, I was married to Zoe, enrolled in a doctoral program at Rutgers, and teaching Social Studies at Junior High #43 on Amsterdam Avenue and 127th Street. As I was walking down Broadway, I happened to stop at a corner newsstand and picked up a copy of Downbeat. There on the cover, were the words: "Is Bobby Darin the next Sinatra?" I couldn't believe it. That was the Bobby Walden Cassotto I once had ushered with, his face blazing with triumph from the glossy page of the tabloid. I rushed home to tell Zoe, and as soon as we could rushed to see Darin at the Copa. He animated the room with an electric magnetism that mesmerized the crowd, holding them enthralled. His voice was a steam engine hidden within a caress, sweet words that didn't camouflage the pumping engine of raw sex, the urgency of lust and transcendence floated across the room, everything releasing as waves of applause cascaded over him. Zoe suggested we go back to say hello to him after the show. "I'm sure he'll remember you," she insisted. But I wasn't feeling good about my position in life at that moment. I wasn't achieving what I wanted to and felt ashamed and dwarfed, being in such close proximity to his rising celebrity, his magnetism. I dreamt of glory, becoming a psychoanalyst, making an important contribution to the world. The irony is that Darin had always been supportive of me, slapping me on the back with a brotherly camaraderie, saying, "You'll make it Kap. You'll do it." My life seemed meager and disappointing. I fumbled, making excuses to

Zoe that we'd do it another time. I was young enough then, not to understand the tricks and betrayals of time. That we don't have forever to say the things that we mean to say, to complete the puzzle that lies before us. That good friends don't care how many degrees you have or what your stock holdings are. In 1973, following his second open heart surgery, Bobby Darin died at age thirty-seven. I never got that chance to see him again.

Suzanne took the message of that story to heart. Throughout our marriage she never failed to remind me, as she had at the party where we met, "Don't wait. There's no time like the present."

Suzanne and I were not that young at the time we married. She was 38, and I was 47. She had a way of connecting to the boy in me, who likes to joke around in the proverbial playground, gently insulting his friends and making the most of his own sexuality. The boy grows up to be a guy, not really a man. The "man" is the image he projects at work, not at home. At home he sometimes likes to talk to his wife as if they were in a Bogart movie. He wants to stay young and playful. I'd put on the Doors and croon along with Morrison singing, "Do you love her madly? Do you need her badly?" – swinging my hips like a Dionysian lizard king. Suzanne would clap her hands and cheer me on, rooting for me like a groupie at the Fillmore West.

We traveled to Orgonon, the museum of Wilhelm Reich, the radical psychiatrist who wrote *The Function of the Orgasm*. Suzanne celebrated my unconventionality, including my interest in the radical thought that most of the psychoanalytic world found too far beyond the mainstream Freudian couch. She understood my need to feel young, and she spoke to that part of me – urging it forward and asking what it wanted. Suzanne, too, wanted to feel young again, but she had a stronger need to be adored, cherished, and loved. She wanted to be made to feel precious, like those pearls, diamonds, and emeralds that she loved. She didn't want me to buy her a lot of expensive items, only a select few things that spoke to her essence.

In a chapter entitled "*What Does the Soul Want?*" James Hillman cites a letter from a woman to the man she is seeing:

> You ask what I want. I need your companionship as you need mine. I want your love and devotion. You must dedicate your life to me and in return I will give myself to you. But you must discover how to come closer to me. … Put soul in your writing. Why not let your imagination run wild again?

A soul wants its soul mate to imagine its deepest needs into being and devise ways of responding to those needs. The soul wants to be valued, but it wants the other person to discover – not be told – what it wants. The soul wants to be loved, but leaves it to the other to know how to bestow this love. The soul wants to be understood, but it entrusts the other with the responsibility of reaching that understanding.

What I mean by understanding, in the sense that the soul craves it, is touching of the loved one's deepest recesses. We all project images of ourselves and the life we want, and we want our partner to speak to those images, to imagine life as we imagine it. Suzanne approached life as an explorer, seeking out adventure wherever she could find it. At the beginning, we traveled a great deal, roaming the world together, and when we weren't actually traveling, we planned future trips to ever more exotic places.

Soul is the poetry of the mind – fantasies or images of the beloved and projections for the future. It is the way we imagine the world around us, the depth of feeling and imaginative capacity we have for the other person. Suzanne possessed this depth of feeling. It was apparent in the way she listened, how she locked her attention around what the other person was saying. Friends repeatedly remarked on the depth of interest they experienced emerging from her. Under her compassionate gaze their deepest secrets, darkest dreams, and hidden wishes emerged.

Chapter Nine

Put Your Dreams Away

In time I grew to view myself as stranded on an island of my new life, existing at times with a woman who had become a stranger. She was someone I once knew and loved with passion. Yet she had gone. In her place existed someone who resembled her, but was not her, a woman who constantly reminded me of an earlier version of herself, who was a once source of life and vitality.

In "Personality Death, Object Loss, and the Uncanny," the psychoanalyst Carolyn Feigelson elaborates on the idea of the uncanny. The core of Suzanne's center had been violated. When I looked at her, I saw the same person she had been, but always encountered eerie images that shifted back and forth between that person and the current one, between Suzanne in the past and Suzanne in the present. Sometimes I saw Suzanne during the early years of our marriage, reaching up to serve a tennis ball at the courts in Central Park, filled with the pleasure of the budding spring, the natural athletic grace of her body, stretching like a feline. Then the vision would burn away as I considered the overweight woman lying on the couch, trembling, drooling, beseeching.

Feigelson's husband sustained a serious head injury, and as a result his entire personality altered radically. She writes that the "eerie effect comes from the awareness of one person within another; another existence going on, something remote, or something violent, or just something profoundly missing. ...How is it possible to lose half a person?"

We have all looked at pictures of the people we love when they were young and been struck by how time's tide has transformed them. Hair turned gray or receding, lines etched into the contour of the face, muscles sagging. These changes occur gradually, over time. We hardly notice them in a person we live with, or in ourselves.

When people we have known for years don't recognize us or forget what role we played in their lives, or even the role they themselves played in life, we are thrown off balance. We ask, "Who are these people?"

At first, I was terrified of how the disease ate away at Suzanne. Her loss of mobility and body tone, her mood changes and weight gain, her general malaise and disengagement from the world left me feeling cheated of the woman I had loved and married. Disability ushers in a new language of love, composed of revised or amended feelings and diminished hopes. I resented the changes I saw. What had happened to the person I once knew and loved? How could the woman I had been so attracted to change so drastically before my eyes? In a slow, frightening process, Suzanne became someone I wasn't always sure I recognized.

Her constant, demoralizing fatigue played havoc with that and disrupted the harmony of our everyday life. The timbre of our conversations changed. Where they once had flowed without effort, they now ran in spurts and starts, depending on how tired Suzanne was, how much her speech slurred, and how difficult it was for her to concentrate. After a few years it wasn't just her legs that were paralyzed. Her entire internal system had gone awry. Sometimes I looked her straight in the eye and wondered if I knew her. At other times I was overcome by the eerie sensation that I was existing with a person I didn't know or want and desperately wanted the person I once knew and could no longer have. We had planned a life with rich expectations. What had happened to that life, and who was this person I was left with? She was like a reminder of her former self – someone I once loved, but now loved differently. I needed the strength to live with the uncertainty of what she might become.

How much can one person tolerate? People with disabilities face sharp psychological reactions, ranging from depressive responses to apathy or phases of intense withdrawal. Over the course of Suzanne's MS, she wrestled with breast cancer, the loss of mobility, two shoulder replacements and encroaching cognitive impairment. How could she not lapse into a depression, mourning the loss of her autonomy, her assertive body and agile mind? And how could she bear the realization that her condition was permanent – that the self she had lost would never return?

Gradually, I realized that Suzanne's disability was affecting her cognitive functioning. During the last six or seven years of her illness, she groped for words, could not listen to me as closely as she once had, and often did not remember what we had discussed only the day before. A woman who once could size up a situation in a flash now just didn't seem to "get it." And she was always tired.

We went to the play, *Dinner at Eight*. The protagonist pawned his watch to pay a hotel bill. Afterwards as I was wheeling her home, I tried to discuss the play with her and realized how this once brilliant woman had not grasped the plot. I asked her why she thought he removed his watch and put it on the table.

"I'm not sure," she shrugged. This was a moment when the uncanny asserted itself -- when it seemed we were living in parallel worlds and the link between us was eroding.

As I wheeled her up Broadway, she observed with a trace of sorrow, "I'm forgetting things, and I don't understand things like I used to. My mind is slowing down."

I couldn't deny this. "We'll make up for it in other ways," I promised her. I learned that touch, massage, the even rhythm of my fingers in her hair soothed her at a profound nonverbal level. As opposed to a radical feisty adolescent, I saw her now as a magnificent infant – trusting, vulnerable, and lost in a world of sensory impressions.

I remember speaking with a friend of mine who had suffered a stroke a few years earlier. He had had a brilliant mind and was a highly regarded English teacher at City College. He told me it took him a good eight months after his stroke to feel confident enough to go back to teaching. The challenge wasn't just learning how to compensate for the cognitive functioning he had lost, it was coming to accept the fact that he had lost it. Some nimble, vital part of his brain – a part he had loved and identified with – was gone forever. "I'm not as quick on my feet as I used to be," he confided and his dark gray eyes flooded with despair. "My teaching abilities will never be the same."

"I don't like talking in front of people any more. I know I slur some words and have trouble finding others. I'm only comfortable talking with one person at a time."

I suggested she just go slowly.

"But people won't wait for me to get the words out," she replied. "They get impatient and start talking among themselves."

I knew this was often true, and it made Suzanne feel like a social outcast. I encouraged Suzanne to tell me about these humiliations. There is something deeply consoling and empowering about putting one's feelings into words, even if no solution to the problem can be found.

The changes that occurred in Suzanne came about gradually, over a period of nineteen years, but they first appeared when she was in the prime of her life. I resented them not only for limiting her mobility and scope of interests, but also for limiting our lives. Where once we had free-ranging and lively discussions, Suzanne now was forced to focus almost exclusively on the minutiae of coping with disease. How a new pill was working, or the side effects it was causing. The new anxiety about a tremor in her arm that was increasing. Her fear that she had forgotten how to operate the buttons of the tape recorder. Toward the end of her life, I would call her four or five times a day so she could report on how she was feeling at the moment. Our conversations came to revolve around how she had managed, with the help of Lenore or Mana, to dress and to eat, to transfer from bed to wheelchair and from wheelchair to reclining chair in front of the television set, how unhappy she was, if the weather was inclement, that she couldn't go outside and feel the air on her face, and how she longed to escape the confinement of our apartment.

Her disability was my concern as well. But these conversations – so limited compared to the conversations we used to have – sometimes made me feel as if I were talking to a woman who the fates had pushed backwards into childhood where the most concrete details of her day became a universe within themselves. I often came home from work to find her withdrawn and apathetic. It was then that I grew most resentful, not of Suzanne, but of the illness that had put her in this state. Occasionally I lost my temper and blurted out nasty thoughts.

Once I attacked her with my words. "You know, you're getting to be a burden." My words were like hard small turds, stinking up the room. I wanted to swallow them back, but I couldn't.

Her mouth opened like a wound in her face. "If you want to leave me, go ahead. I'll just have to try to find someone else."

I was instantly filled with remorse, knowing how deeply I had hurt her. Realistically, she had no way of finding someone else. She couldn't even leave the apartment unattended.

"I'd never leave you, you dope." Tears prevented my vision. "Don't ever think that. You know it's just my impatience speaking. Forget it, if you can. Or tell me to go to hell."

Whatever temper tantrums I pitched came out of intolerable feelings of helplessness. But they were over quickly, and I always apologized on the spot. Still, I seemed confronted with two choices: attempt to draw Suzanne out or let her lapse into a kind of sluggishness. Making the choice involved a continual conflict. In some ways, it was easier to let her lapse, for then I didn't have to make the enormous effort it took to draw her out.

At first, I was not willing to accept the permanence of Suzanne's condition. I didn't want to face the fact that she would never again be the wife I once had. But that was not something I could deny for long, and the more I came to accept it, the more I was able to help her. I sought out ways to turn her interests away from herself and back to the world around her, in which she had once taken such passionate interest. I rented films of the operas she most loved, so she could listen to the music she adored while training her mind to follow the familiar plots. I brought her books I thought would interest her, and when her eyes failed, I read to her aloud from them.

The challenge was trying to ascertain how much the stimulation pleased her and distracted her, and how much it reinforced her sense of deficit. Suzanne's eyes sometimes rewarded me with a brilliant flash of recognition. But, at other times, the slow current of the disease pulled her under. "I've Got You Under My Skin" pulsed through the annals of memory. Outside the window was a view of the New York skyline and a grid of square yellow lights in gray pre-war buildings. The color of old homes. "So deep in my heart, you are a part of me. ... you fool, you never can win. I sat in a middle room alone, drinking coffee, learning the language of loss, desire, nostalgia and hope. "Time is so old, and love so brief. Love is pure gold, and time a thief." The lyrics of songs poured from the radio. Suzanne slept in the next room, in the next world, dreams flickering beneath her eyelids – visions of the great bear and the swollen mind.

Late in her illness, Suzanne became furious with me for not planning a cruise to Alaska. "You know I've always wanted to go there," she insisted. "And you promised to take me. But damn it, Harv, I haven't seen you do the first thing about it." I looked at her in utter astonishment. "If you're not going to take me," she went on, "I'll just have to go with Lenore."

The thought of flying to California, transferring her from the plane to the hotel, from the hotel to the cruise ship, and repeating the whole process in reverse on the way back to New York was daunting. So many things could go wrong. What if she had to use the restroom during the cross-country flight? Her wheelchair wouldn't make it up the aisle. What the hell would make her to want to take such a trip?

I knew she wasn't crazy. She was a woman who refused to give up her dreams – a woman who maintained her stubborn belief that she could do whatever she wanted, with the smallest modicum of help. She could slay the mightiest dragon. This courageous, if obstinate, attitude emanated from her and when it appeared it never failed to astound me. I often thought of her battered body as a graceful boat caught in wild ocean currents and smashed by the tide against the rocks, finding relief as the tide receded, then getting pummeled again as the tide crashed on the shores of her ravaged body.

I vowed to take her to Alaska as soon as she recovered from the surgery that was supposed to resolve her urinary problems. But like Eurydice at the moment Orpheus turned, Neptune pulled her back into the underworld forever. We began the delicate pas-de-deux formed of our years together.

Suzanne rarely showed anger. When I asked her about this, she didn't see it that way. That day her eyes splashed with brilliance:

> What's the point of feeling like a victim? I know your friends think I should be angrier about what's happening to me, but what the hell good would that do? Yes, I feel betrayed. By nature, by what I inherited, by the genes that were given to me at birth. But does that mean I should be angry with my parents for giving me those genes? Can't you see that wouldn't get me anywhere? Besides, do you want to be married to an angry woman? Is that who you think I am? Someone who's mad all the time, but not expressing it?

Because I'm quiet or subdued doesn't mean I don't feel like hell about this. Look at me, for God's sake! Listen, Harv, everything I've read about this disease – and you know I've read a lot – tells me that anger actually induces feelings of helplessness. It doesn't overcome them. When you're angry at something that you can't do anything about, it makes you feel weak and passive. I know that's true. I still have enough marbles to reason that out. What do you want from me? I need somehow to find peace for myself. I have to find contentment in what I can do for myself, not rage about what I can't do.

Sometimes my anger, and not Suzanne's lack of it, was the problem. I became enraged when Suzanne fell, as she did more and more often. She called me on it. "What gets you so angry when I'm the one who has all the trouble getting around?" I explained the misery of my helplessness when I had trouble lifting her up. Feeling helpless has always made me furious. But I assured her I was working on a solution. I was going to the health club three times a week and lifting weights. Suzanne had a better idea. She suggested I meet her physical therapist at the MS Center at Roosevelt Hospital so he could demonstrate his method of lifting her off the floor.

I was thrilled at the prospect. The fifth floor physical therapy room was a large white space with green rubber mats on the floor. The institutional air smelled of fungus mixed with detergents. The soft sensuous sound of fists gently massaging flesh, and the soft low grunting of patients lifting themselves on bars filled the air. Suzanne and Lenore stood off to one side, near a mirror. For a moment, seen in profile, Suzanne appeared normal again, and the vision of her from ten years earlier pulsed before me. Then Suzanne's trainer – a sliver of a man with dark expressive eyes – pumped my hand, welcoming me, pulling me out of my reverie.

"How do you lift her?" he inquired.

"I first try to raise her to a hassock and transfer her from there to a chair." I decided not to tell him that sometimes I had to get the superintendent to give me a hand.

"There is a better way of going about it. Let me show you." He positioned Suzanne on the floor and stretched her legs wide in the shape of a V. Then he encircled her body with his arms, positioning his shoulders beneath her armpits. He lodged his knee between her legs. I watched with skepticism as his lifting motions produced no results. He tried again, and then continued struggling as Suzanne's limp body wrestled in his arms, unable to move. I averted my eyes from his futility, imagining I could make him feel like less of a failure. But when I looked again, a vein protruded from his earnest forehead as he continued his struggle, unwilling to concede defeat. A wave of shame rose in my stomach. After all, they were a team, and if one lost, so did the other.

"Would you mind supervising me while I give it a try?"

He agreed at once and got up off the floor. I lowered myself to the mat and grabbed Suzanne from behind, positioning her precariously on the edge of the cushion. I lifted her onto a stool, then rested, grateful for the vast space, unlike the small rooms of our apartment filled with furniture and fragile bric-a-brac.

"Now I'm going to lift her onto that chair." I tried for the chair in question and managed to seat her.

"How was that?"

"Not bad," he replied. "To tell you the truth, I think you have it down pretty well. I don't think you need any other strategy."

"Thanks" I was careful not to look to Suzanne, afraid we might start laughing. I didn't want our shared compact of humor to humiliate this man who was trying so hard to help her and whom she relied on. We both made certain to appear humble and grateful.

As my love for Suzanne shifted from passionate romance to intense concern, I helped her hold onto as much happiness and self-esteem as she could. When the tide came in, we could dream of vacations to Rome and Athens, trips to the moon on the wings of our love, even voyages to Alaska. When the tide was out, everything slowed down and the plot became static. Her ability to find joy in the world diminished, and I feared that her day-to-day existence would become no more than a rite of survival. I filled the house with Puccini arias, fresh cut flowers, Greek pastries and fresh baked rugelah. I made plans to get together with those people who were patient with Suzanne and didn't ask that she be the life of the party. In the country we discovered two new and rare friends, Gail and Marty. Soon they were coming over to our place every Friday and Saturday night. They were understanding and gracious with Suzanne, they made her feel inclined to have even more company. Gradually, we invited Candace and Domingo and a few other people to join our circle, and eventually we became a gang of loving friends, all of whom cherished Suzanne. When we added Al to the mix, I was able to have a cigar with them and discuss music and old films, subjects we both loved and enjoyed quizzing each other about. At the end of our evenings, Gail would often sit and talk quietly with Suzanne. Then the two of them would watch *Law and Order* reruns before Suzanne tired and needed to be helped to bed.

Friends used to tell me, "Suzanne will be okay, you know. She's a fighter." But what did this mean? Didn't it imply that she had some control over the course of her disease? Both Suzanne and I knew this was not the case.

"Yes, I'm a fighter," she would say. "But I'm not fighting the disease, I'm fighting its desire to pull me into a deep depression. That would be the end of me. It's bad enough as it is, Harv, I'm not going to give it the power to destroy me."

For most people, taking action, doing anything, is far more acceptable than remaining passive. The belief that acceptance demonstrates passivity while raging and fighting demonstrates strength, is seductive, – if we only fight hard enough we are guaranteed a triumphant ending. But as the chaos narrative unfolds, the reality is that fighting isn't useless, but requires a radical redefinition: one learns to shift the fight away from recovery towards acceptance. As Barbara Webster writes, "Activity, doing something about it, rests on the understanding that nature can be controlled, something can always be done, and tomorrow will be better than today. Highlighting future implies the possibility and efficacy of action."

Mae West, that ornery pistol who defied the Hollywood conventions of femininity with the power of her sheer life force, once exclaimed, "You get what you take. No limits!" I fantasized about Mae West bursting out of the TV set, rising up majestically in our living room, and telling people the rules of the road. "The world is a proposition. If you don't come on to it, you get tuned down."

When well-intentioned friends and relatives spoke of Suzanne's indomitable spirit, her unwillingness to give up, they failed to grasp that the progression and outcome of the disease were not in her hands. It might be nice to believe that "fighting" her illness would put it within her control, but Suzanne and I learned early on the pain of succumbing to this illusion.

Suzanne understood that she had to integrate MS into her life – not ignore it, minimize it, or claim that she could beat it, much as she may have wanted to. She had to accept the limitations the illness imposed on her and turn her back on the cultural values of our society that speak of hard work, fighting the good fight, and beating the odds. I would recast the notion of battling a disease as one of negotiating with disease. Suzanne's efforts attempts to overcome the shame at her incontinence, the humiliation at her slurring of words, and the depression over being skirted to the fringes of society, constituted her true fight and most stunning victories.

Of course, Suzanne had moments of wanting to hide from the world. Nor does acceptance preclude anger. Suzanne's anger may have been muted, and she was frustrated over not being able to do the simple things most of us take for granted, like walking a block or two, buttoning a blouse, or writing a note to a friend. But she never allowed multiple sclerosis to totally shatter her life, yet she never harbored false hopes either. She knew that even if science discovered a cure for MS, it would be too late for her. But her will to live and to turn life to her advantage as much as possible always amazed and inspired me.

One day she said, "I've gone down the Colorado river in a raft in high season, with the water surging in my face. Do you know what that's like?"

"Tell me about it."

"If I can do that, I can contend with this." She lounged back into green leather sofa. Splinters of white winter light crept in from behind the drapes. That afternoon her face was filled with electricity, her lips moistened and her eyes glowed, vivid with the experience. "You feel like your whole life is surging up into your throat. Any obstacle may be the end, a void, oblivion. But the harder the river runs, the more twists and turns it throws at you, the higher you sit. It's like you know that you're really fighting something more than just survival. You're proving who you are."

One summer afternoon we drove to Chattaqua, an adult educational community at the edge of New York State. It was warm and the trees were glistening a deep verdant green, exuding the obscene fecundity of life. Suzanne put on a CD of Maria Callas singing La Traviata. She sung of the fallen woman, dying of tuberculosis with the dollar bills sticking to her skin as the bourgeois family rush in, too late, to recant and recognize her glory. The voice rose and crested in my chest like a claw, then like a fist.

"I can't listen to this. It's just too much to feel."

"What are you running away from?" asked Suzanne.

"I can't explain." The dying woman, the illness, the music tearing through my head flooded me. "Honey, if I feel this much voltage I'll drive the car off the road."

That night before we fell asleep Suzanne kissed me. "Is this too much for you to feel?" The question hung heavy in the air between us, and I stroked her creamy skin, and kissed her petulant lips into silence and then we both drifted into a peaceful dreamless sleep.

For as long as Suzanne lived, no matter how much despair she encountered, her support and encouragement continued to remain active in everything I did. She wanted me to be happy and find my true calling in life. "Whatever you do," she insisted, "Whether it's therapy or writing, you better leave some part in it for me to play. I'll be there, somehow, helping you."

I used to tell my analyst that I wanted to emerge from therapy less restricted, but not too sane. Sanity was for those who couldn't risk anything. As I spoke, my analyst's expensive leather shoes creaked against each other as she listened to me.

At home Suzanne challenged this. "What makes you think doing what you want is so crazy?" she asked, curled up beside me, stroking my razor stubble with long elegant fingers. "Taking risks and making the world into your playground – that's what I call sanity, Harv."

She was enthusiastic about my folly of wanting to play piano. It was much too late in life for me to have any hope of mastering the instrument, but she thought it was a wonderful idea and urged me to get the best upright on the market. I bought a Yamaha made with an elegant dark mahogany wood and set about applying my middle-aged fingers to the elusive mystery of the black and white keys, wanting to summon up the playful insouciance of Rodgers and Hart. After three years I accepted what I had known all along – that my fingers had lost dexterity and I was fumbling through simple versions of Broadway musicals. Now what was I supposed to do? Sell the Yamaha and, because of its depreciation, lose a considerable amount of money? I've always had a problem selling items at a loss.

"Let go of it, Harv," Suzanne advised. "You've tried. It's fine. There are so many other things in the world for you to do. Don't get stuck on this. Just tango on." She reached for me from the wheel chair and drew her hand down my arm. Then her fingers found the strength to weave themselves into mine. Then I had an idea. My first wife, Zoe, was an accomplished pianist. I tentatively asked Suzanne how she would feel if I offered the piano to Zoe. "Great idea!" A smile dappled through her sagging skin.

And so over the years as Suzanne's body withered her spirit stirred me, inflamed me, and transformed me into a different man. I started bicycling for the MS fundraiser, taking a thirty-mile trip around Manhattan. I started writing differently – not about what I thought people wanted to hear, but what I found I wanted to express. I feel her here now, in these memories, in these stories, in these pages.

Chapter Ten

I'll Never Smile Again

In 1989 I was teaching a course at NPAP about psychoanalytic technique. We were reading *The Analytic Attitude*, in which Roy Schafer amplifies the concept of the "second self." This psychoanalytic formulation explains why, in our professional capacity as analysts, we exhibit beneficent qualities that are absent from our everyday interactions. Schafer extends this concept to performing artists, writers, and painters. Schafer speaks of creative artists who demonstrate more admirable qualities during a performance than they ever do in their daily lives. He cites creative writers, who, according to their most informed biographers, exhibit more misery, cruelty, greed, snobbery, or self-destructiveness in their day-to-day lives than the average person. Yet, these same people achieve sublime expressions of self-sacrifice, humanity, compassion, and joy in their writing. "Though they are not angels," Schafer asserts, "They write like angels." At their best such writers make us wish we were like them, or that we had them for friends, parents, or lovers, and that in responding to them so enthusiastically we are in fact responding to a representation of how we would like to see ourselves transformed.

After class, a student came up to me, excited by remarks I had dropped in previous classes. She gathered that I had a tremendous fondness for Frank Sinatra as a performer. She bubbled on with excitement about an upcoming conference at Hofstra University on Sinatra and she thought that the idea of the "second self" could easily be applied to him. His performance personality was tender, even sentimental – significantly different from the brash, tough, sometimes cruel, persona he exhibited off-stage. She suggested that we submit a joint proposal on the "second self" and Sinatra.

I was invited to present my paper at this conference. Suzanne's eyes glowed as she shared in my triumph. "This is what you've been looking for – a chance to do what you've always wanted to do with Sinatra and at the same make a professional contribution."

As I was preparing for the conference, Sinatra died. The last rhythmic pulsing of his cells gave way. Perhaps a light on the other side welcomed him into heaven. Only the lonely knows.

His death inspired me to work harder on my paper and cited Sinatra's songs to highlight crucial points. I practiced delivering it to Suzanne. Her eyes bathed me with acceptance as she snuggled down into the armchair and struggled to clap her hands. I choked up, flooded with memories of my mother and brother, who were also Sinatra fans. Now all three were dead.

I remember my mother lying in her death bed in Bronx Lebanon, drugged and shrinking into a collection of bones against the starched white sheets – her eyes not seeing me or understanding who I was. Sinatra sang of longing and absence, and I resurrected my mother, the smell of expensive perfume, her secret indulgence. I head her singing, "I'll Never Smile Again Until I Smile at You," as she walked through our cramped apartment, dusting and waiting for my father to return so she could kiss or berate him for his latest hair-brained scheme. I saw my brother in the ICU, plugged up with tubing, his skin green from the lack of oxygen. His aorta had exploded, and he gasped for air. I gripped his hand, trying to send life into his dying body. "Please, stay with me. I'm hungry for your love, for your acknowledgement. See me one more time before you go."

Later on I presented my paper at my Institute. Suzanne insisted on accompanying me, despite the steps at the front of the building. We arrived early and a friend helped me lift her in her wheelchair up the steps to the elevator. I moved Suzanne from her wheelchair to a seat on the aisle. A large crowd had gathered to hear the talk. Jokingly, I said to the moderator, "I never knew I was so popular."

As I delivered my paper, I kept looking at Suzanne. Every time I met her eyes, I could sense her love and admiration. I flushed with excitement at the flicker of her old independence and her passion for music still throbbing within her body. For a few hours she was able to burn off a great mantle of fog. It was a spectacular evening for me. Even today, when I think back on it, I can feel the hair rise on the back of my neck.

As she descended further into the disease, her past support buttressed me and enabled me to focus my energies almost entirely on her. A level of concern and free-floating apprehension –which had never been part in her outlook on life – seeped into the air between us. We tried to go on with life as usual but we knew the disease was taking its incremental toll. One evening she was unable to walk down the hallway to our front elevator. Then she had to use a cane, then two canes, then a walker. A few months after purchasing the first walker, she required a larger, stronger walker. A few months later, she needed an electric scooter. She loved that scooter. She called it her best friend, and for some time she enjoyed zipping around the city in it. When one of her actual best friends, Stan, bought her standing-room seats at the Metropolitan Opera, she was able to travel the ten blocks between our apartment and the opera house and back by herself. But by the late 1990s she could no longer walk or even get out of the chair unassisted.

Over time the prednisone caused her shoulder bones to deteriorate, making it impossible for her to raise her hands above breast-level. This meant she couldn't answer the telephone or feed herself. I thought of filing a malpractice suit, but the lawyer believed too much time had elapsed between cause and consequence. In 1997 Suzanne had to undergo two complete shoulder replacements, each resulting in four weeks of rehabilitation, the first at the Helen Hayes Institute, the second at Burke. She enjoyed the social aspects of Burke and loved it when I visited her on weekends and wheeled her outside, so she could take pleasure in the lush gardens and talk with the other patients, who all sought her out to confide in.

It was springtime. The trees were in the first flush of green, and the earth whispered a promise of summer. We sat by the garden, and I ran a brush through her hair, as my eyes blurred with tears.

She took my hand. "What is it? What's wrong sweetheart?"

At her voice, the lawsuit, the prednisone and the denuded bones all disappeared into the air fragrant with wisteria. "Nothing. I'm only happy."

Through it all, I continued to believe she would outlive me. She was nine years younger and, despite the MS, had a strong constitution. "I want you to be provided for," I told her more than once. "That's why I have life insurance."

"Maybe you'd better take out some more," she answered. "When you go, I think I'll finally take that cruise to Alaska." Her eyes sparkled. To this day I regret not having taken her on that cruise.

About a year before her death, I noticed that Suzanne and Lenore were keeping some kind of secret from me. One night I came home and Suzanne told me to wait in the living room for a moment. "I've got a surprise for you." She signaled to Lenore to wheel her into the bedroom. When they came out, she was wearing a mink jacket.

"Are you crazy?" I asked. "Who wears fur these days?"

"I do," she answered indignantly. "I've always wanted a jacket like this."

"I can't believe you. I think you're nuts."

Suzanne looked at Lenore and burst out laughing. "Didn't I tell you he would react this way? I know him, don't I?" Then she looked back at me and added, "If you had taken me on that cruise to Alaska, I might have waited a year before buying it."

There was no blame in our relationship. Suzanne could have displaced her negative feelings and come to see me as someone acting in the place of her parents who had failed to protect her. Or I might have come to blame Suzanne for bringing MS into our lives and irrevocably disrupting our relationship. Thankfully, neither of us blamed the other. But we saw how blame could creep into a relationship when one partner had a disability. A pervading gloom hung in the atmosphere like poisonous gas.

The first we encountered through our curiosity about bee therapy, which Suzanne and I had been reading about in the MS Quarterly. Bees are collected in a large glass container, then fed into smaller containers, which the MS patients hold against their legs, allowing the bees to sting them. The bees' sting injects a substance into the system that, in some patients, rejuvenates the legs and, if all goes well, increases their mobility.

I thought this had interesting possibilities and mentioned it one day when we were out in Montague to a couple who had come by for a visit. Our friend Dottie said that she knew of someone who lived only about a mile away, had MS, and did bee therapy. I was excited about the coincidence and asked Suzanne if she'd be willing to meet this woman. Suzanne was somewhat less enthusiastic but agreed to an initial meeting. We got the woman's address and phone number and made plans to visit the next day.

The woman's daughter greeted us at the door. She had moved to the area to be close to her mother. Inside this split-level ranch house, the first thing we noticed were dozens of bees buzzing about in a large glass container. The house was unkempt and the woman we had come to see was confined to a wheelchair. She could not have been more gracious as she welcomed us to her home. She told us that she was paralyzed and could not walk at all, but had found some improvement through the use of the bee therapy. After the bees stung her, she claimed to feel movement in her legs. At least she could move them apart a bit, whereas before she had not been able to do even that. A pile of dead bees lay on her kitchen table. Suzanne wasn't perturbed by the presence of the bees, and I thought if she could get around the unpleasant aspects of the treatment, there might be some hope for her in this procedure. Our hostess did point out that she had experienced better results at the outset of the treatment. Her daughter made us some coffee and, although the conversation revolved exclusively around MS, we had a relaxed afternoon – until the husband came home.

His presence made us immediately uncomfortable. It was clear that he resented having a discussion of multiple sclerosis take place in his house. In fact, he seemed to resent his wife for having an illness that brought bees into his life. He seemed to resent us, too, for being interested in his wife's plight. And while I understood his anger, I wished he could have controlled it better. He talked to his wife as if her disease were an insult to him – a burden he didn't wish to bear. His wife was a lovely woman, who just wanted to be loved and appreciated.

After this cursory greeting, he grunted to her that he was going to town later. His eyes were inflamed brown beads pulsing in a bloated face. She winced as he walked out and slammed the door. That she rearranged her features as if by a supreme act of will, and offered us more coffee and cookies. She reminded me of dogs I'd seen in animal shelters with good, sad eyes, asking only for a home and to be of service.

At some point in the conversation, the husband walked back into the kitchen and simply excused himself and left the house. There goes a man, I thought, who feels betrayed by fate. The irritation in his voice, the abruptness of his movements, his unwillingness to prevent even a veneer of sociability in our presence, indicated that he believed life had dealt him the worst blow he could imagine – save having been diagnosed with MS himself.

On another occasion, I met a woman in the parking lot of K-Mart, about five miles from our New Jersey condo. I stopped to watch in amazement as a van, like mine but a bit larger, rolled out a ramp for a woman in a powered wheelchair. She rode out into the parking lot, turned her wheelchair around, and powered the ramp back up into the metallic black van by remote control. I was struck by how smoothly the operation worked, and the woman was able to do it all by herself. I walked up and introduced myself and told her how impressed I was with her remarkable van, which I had seen advertised in magazines, but had never witnessed in action. She introduced herself as Ann, explaining that she suffered from MS and now lived in Milford, Pennsylvania, across the river from us in Montague. She told me she would love to meet Suzanne and gave me her phone number. We called and arranged to go over later that afternoon. Ann's house sat on a hill overlooking a vast field with a scabby motel and an abandoned golf course, choked with mildew. Ann met us at the door and asked us in, but once we were inside, her friendly manner became anxious and strained. Her house was small, a bit rustic, and with no apparent concessions made for a disabled person. It wasn't easy to move around in the warren of small rooms, and Ann never invited Suzanne to sit anywhere but in her wheelchair.

Ann was almost completely isolated in this location, had only a few acquaintances, and was alone most of the time. Her husband worked long hours as the manager of a food service program and was rarely home. Apparently, they barely conversed.

Instantly, I felt that I understood this man. He reminded me of the husband of the woman experimenting with insect venom, in that he blamed his wife for her condition. We stayed about half an hour and then left. As we were leaving, Ann asked us to call her and we nodded noncommittally.

"She seemed uncomfortable about having us in her house," Suzanne noted on the way home. "It was almost as if she regretted asking us to visit. I wondered why she did? I get the sense her husband brought her out there to live and then had just dumped her. It may seem cold, but I don't think I want to see her again. And she never took our number, so maybe she feels the same way. She may have more mobility than I do with that fancy, automated van of hers, but what good does it do her when she's home alone? I couldn't stand to be that isolated."

"We're lucky," I observed. "We're not letting this make us bitter."

That afternoon the condo seemed wide and welcoming, filled with art and opera and salmon grilling in the kitchen. I set Suzanne up on her chaise lounge, and we talked about upcoming movies. I asked her to tell me about opera. I contemplated her white porcelain skin, the sensual bloom of her mouth. I thought of Ann's frozen face, and an image flashed in my brain of the many houses dotting the turnpike, tiny specks of light visible from an airplane at night. How many contained other versions of Ann?

Obviously, Suzanne and I would have been happier if MS had never entered our lives. Everything would have been different. We would have made other choices, different plans. We would have had more fun in life. Yet once faced with the illness, we couldn't build the rest of our life together on pessimism and despair. We knew what the future held, but it made no sense to live in fear. I thought of Steinbeck's *Grapes of Wrath*, which recounts the painful odyssey of the Joad family, depression-era tenant farmers from Oklahoma's Dust Bowl. Thrown off their land by bankers and land-grabbers, the family was forced on a hard journey toward California, which they believed to be a land of plenty. Physically displaced and exposed to a variety of severe hardships, they remained emotionally and spiritually undefeated. Their struggle was monumental, yet the Joads retained their faith in the future and their optimism about life.

Yet when a disability disrupts your relationship, how can you not feel that life has cheated you? It's pointless to deny that your relationship has radically changed, that you feel envious of all the healthy, able-bodied couples. I recall evenings at our condo in New Jersey when we had invited a few friends over and were all sitting around downstairs, talking and laughing and having a good time. After a while, Suzanne would get tired and want to be helped to bed. I had to transfer her to her wheelchair, put the chair on the lift, help her ride to the top of the stairs where I had to transfer her into another wheelchair and push her into the bedroom. Then I had to take off her clothes and put her in a nightgown. I had to take a warm washcloth and wash her face and hands. I had to move her into bed, raising the back of the bed so she could watch television before she went to sleep. I would then kiss her and tell her that if she needed me, all she had to do was buzz me through the intercom. Then I would walk downstairs and rejoin my friends.

As I walked down the stairs, I could hear them laughing and chatting away and became filled with irritation that I'd had to take this time out to help Suzanne. I disliked having been away from the fun and left out of the conversation for even those few minutes. At times, I believed that my friends couldn't care less about what I was going through. Then I wondered, is that what I wanted from them–sympathy for my plight? And I realized that helping Suzanne up the stairs and into bed had taken maybe fifteen or twenty minutes out of my life. What was that compared to what the MS has taken out of hers? I thought of what it meant to Suzanne to have to leave the party early, to ask for help, to be dependent on me, to feel like a burden on others. It wasn't always easy to see things from her point of view, but I had to put my feelings of resentment in perspective. No matter how difficult life was for me, it was incomparably more difficult for her.

By the time Suzanne could no longer walk, I was prepared for major changes.

Nothing could take me by surprise. I became resigned to the next phase of her illness, and the next, and the next. Of course, I had met others with multiple sclerosis and had observed how the disease progressed in each case. Two people at one of the institutes where Suzanne and I belonged to had MS. One, a woman, did quite well over a long period of time. The other, a man, had to stop working and soon could barely walk across a room. But then the progression of his illness slowed down, and he was better off than Suzanne was at the end of her life. Her disease had continued along an unrelenting progressive path. No one knows why this is so, or why a cure is so slow in coming. No one knows why the disease follows such different courses.

In the later stages of Suzanne's illness, it required tremendous work to reach her soul. I had to push past the eerie sensation of the uncanny, the surrealism of her massively disfigured body laying immobile near a vast collection of pill bottles was still Suzanne. I would make it work by bringing my face close to hers, peering with my eyes into her dark brown irises, trying to summon her up as if from a great depth. I imagined myself as Orpheus, summoning her like Eurydice up from Neptune's depths to the surface of the water where for a few moments her consciousness would flash back into action. People who had known Suzanne earlier in life were often shocked and appalled by her transformation. They invariably asked some version of the question, "Who is she now? This is not the woman I knew."

Only a part of Suzanne was missing, not her entire being. I learned patience, waiting for the gift of those precious seconds when her neurons fired and a flicker of her essence flamed again. I learned the message of the subtle pressure of her fingers, the downward drift of her gaze, signals that she was sinking again.

"We're closer now than we ever were," I sometimes reminded her during her lucid moments, taking her hand and stroking it. Bringing vases of flowers closer to her so she could inhale their nectar, delight in gentian and violet petals. "I don't take you for granted. I value every minute we have together. And in loving you, helping you through this, and trying to make your life as comfortable as possible, my life has taken on a deeper meaning."

I told her that if I had to give a single reason for loving her it would be the way her spirit fights against impossible odds, refusing to lie down and take the injustice of fate. I loved the incredible grace she lavished on the will to live. I loved her heart that refused to panic and that always extended itself beyond its capacity. She knew what she was up against, yet she rose above it and never reconciled herself to defeat. When I watched her spirit fight on, I was filled with wonder, for when she fully engaged in the fight, she came as close to perfection as I have ever seen.

I used to daydream about the old movie Magnificent Obsession. The protagonist Bob is an idler, partly responsible for the accidental death of Helen's husband, a former doctor and a man who was revered by his friends and colleagues. After her husband's death, Helen is blinded in a freak accident. Bob gives up his wastrel ways and dedicates himself to medicine. He becomes an ophthalmologist and, without revealing his true identity to Helen, contacts her. They soon fall in love. When Helen eventually finds out who he is, she leaves him. But some time later,

Bob is given an opportunity to restore Helen's sight. He performs an operation brilliantly, and Helen sees again. Wow, I thought, if only I could find a cure for MS, then I would be a hero like Bob. Such fantasies would flood my mind when I thought of all the men I knew whose wives didn't have MS. I couldn't help but resent them for their easy lives. How would they fare, I wondered, if they had to deal with what I was facing? In most cases, I thought they wouldn't do as well, so it probably was better that I was the one. I had the strength to cope with it.

At times I heard Suzanne's voice crying, "Save me. Just save me from this." When I first met her, that voice had cried, "Love me. Just love me." I could still love her and keep her temporarily safe, but I couldn't save her from her disease. That's for the movies, not real life. As much as I loved her, I could not heal her. This often brought me to tears.

Some evenings I'd play a Cole Porter song for Suzanne:

> I love you
> Hums the April breeze.
> I love you
> Echo the hills.
> I love you
> The golden dawn agrees
> ...
> I love you,
> That's the song of songs
> And it all belongs
> To you and me.

We cultivated our love, beating back the gloom of the New York winter. I'd always finish the piece with a challenge: "Beats opera any day."

"Oh yeah?" Suzanne would shoot back, pretending to glare. "Not for me it doesn't."

Saving Beauty

I sat in the hospital in a chair by her bed, with a variety of forms and medical decisions, I was so alone with this decision. The fate of disconnecting her. Her hair still glorious, spilling out around her in the bed. And the uncanny body that was bloated and disfigured beyond recognition heaving against the black mouth of night.

Chapter Eleven

Moonlight Becomes You

When Suzanne contracted the pseudomonas infection following her surgery at New York Hospital, the doctors tried to have her perform respiratory exercises. They brought a plastic contraption, which reminded me of the device used to pick lottery winners, into her hospital room. The patient breathes into a tube to raise three plastic balls to strengthen her lungs. When Suzanne tried to puff, there was only a wheezing sound. Her lungs were failing, and I was shocked by the shallowness of her breathing. During visiting hours she could only address her friend by nodding her head. Even at the end of her life, Suzanne wanted to make people around her comfortable. She struggled to use her remaining lung capacity to speak and reassure them. I put my lips to her ear and told her that we would have to practice raising those plastic balls–that it would just take time. The doctor watched me. His masked features could not hide his limited optimism.

Outside the room he spoke to me quietly explaining that Suzanne's lungs lacked the capacity to resume normal functioning. She would not be able to breathe on her own if the respirator were removed. In the surreal blur of the metallic hospital corridors, smelling of disinfectants and the buzzing with the noise of machines. I wondered how long she could continue. Might her lung capacity increase? Might she eventually be able to breathe without the machine?

I could still hear Suzanne's gasping in the other room, like a fish, gutted, struggling on the boards of the fisherman's boat.

'What about her living will? She's already been intubated."

"Once the committee reviews the case and sees whether she has any hope of regaining pulmonary function, then it's up to you as the next of kin."

Kin. Faith. Death. There was not a round dark sanctuary of prayer for me to fall into and find solace. The halls of the hospital reduced everything to equations, antibiotics, dosing schedules, blood, gases and probable outcomes. If Suzanne had been older, if the MS had been more severely advanced, this situation would have followed a simpler scenario. The tubes would never have been inserted. The process would not have been set in motion.

I walked back to Suzanne's bedside. Psychiatrists in white coats had made rounds earlier and tried to get her to speak by squeezing her hands. They got nowhere. The movement of her hands was erratic and then stopped as she slipped into a semi-coma.

Friends who came to visit didn't stay long enough to discuss the issue of withdrawing life support with me. I didn't want them to. I knew they would support me in whatever decision I made. If I decided it was wrong to take her off the respirator, who would disagree? If I decoded it was wrong to keep her on it and force her to go on living, chained to a machine, who would argue with me? I sat in the metallic pavilion overlooking the Hudson River. The water was gray like liquid lead. The incision where the surgeon had attempted to insert the ileal chimney had left a gaping hole in Suzanne's abdomen. The doctors spoke in jargon about abscesses and how the antibiotics weren't working because her immune system was shutting down.

Caroline accompanied me to the meeting with the head of the ICU. The canes, the wheelchairs, the avalanche of medications, the progressive paralysis were all part of a web, and we were standing in the center. The doctors had stopped administering antibiotics. After all Suzanne had endured during the last five weeks in the hospital – the steady loss of strength as she battled the raging infection, the advancing paralysis, the weakening of her lungs, the increasing difficulty in drawing breath – was it reasonable to imagine that she would ever come home? Could I let her go on living with no possibility of ever moving or breathing on her own again? Was it more humane to set her free? And if I did that, would it be for her sake or for mine? I was not prepared to see my wife die. Intellectually, I had always grasped her mortality, but I needed to believe she would outlive me. Perhaps this was my own fantasy of avoiding abandonment. I still clung to the image of Suzanne as a widow in a nursing home back in Baltimore –somehow happy despite the odds.

"I can't imagine letting her go on in that condition indefinitely," I confided to Caroline. "She's a prisoner of the machine."

"I know she wouldn't want to live that way, Dad." She put her arm around me. I surrendered to her wisdom, her straight A's at the Bronx High School of Science, her sensible shoes, the comfort of her love, uncomplicated like pumpernickel bread. She shook her head, framed with straight black hair cut in the modern style, like a bowl, with firm authority. "She's not going to get any better. The doctors all agree on that. Why subject her to this? It's not fair to her. Or to you."

I wrestled with the decision for a week. I went over it again and again in my mind. I spent long hours at Suzanne's bedside each day, asking her silent questions, trying to glean her answers from a possible flash of recognition. Three of her closest friends continued to come to the hospital regularly, but Suzanne remained lost to the outside world, suspended in a delirious somnolence. I wondered if she was aware of their presence.

I was distressed that Suzanne had no family with whom I might discuss the decision. Her brother, Fred, never showed any interest in coming to the hospital to see his sister. Her father had died about seven years before from a congestive heart condition, and her mother had died two years ago. Both her parents had been in an assisted living facility, then were moved separately to emergency accommodations where they died. Her father could barely breathe at the end of his life, and her mother had lingered for months in a coma. Suzanne had watched them suffer slowly until they expired. She was relieved at her parents' death. I wondered what part of me that would experience relief if Suzanne was finally detached from the respirator. I wondered whether the desire to pursue a better life for myself, freed from the burdens of Suzanne's illness, played a part in my decision.

"We're not talking about your life, Dad." Caroline was firm. "We're talking about hers. Look at what she's had to go through all these years. This seems like the final insult."

That week Caroline stuck close by me. Yet she allowed me my own space as well. I met her one evening for dinner. I wanted to get her perspective about Suzanne's condition.

"It's been so hard for so long. Her right hand shook so much that it made is practically impossible for her to hold a fork." Caroline remembered, her eyes moist with emotion. "I remember how easily she tired after socializing. Maybe it was because her speech slurred and her patience with herself became diminished?"

"I wonder how you feel about this?"

"Dad, at first she had to walk with a cane. And it seemed like she was proud of herself. I know she missed smoking and she told me that you bought her cigarillos so she would be able to give up cigarettes. But then with the cigarillo she cut quite a figure for herself. Actually it was quite glamorous. She exuded a certain kind of sophistication."

"How did you feel when she could no longer use the cane?"

"Well it wasn't the cane that got to me. When she started using the walker I began to feel embarrassed. I felt almost ashamed to walk in the street with her. I hated the walker and I didn't want anyone to see Suzanne with it. So I found myself making excuses for not taking a walk with her for fear we would run into someone she knew. I don't know why I felt that way, I was an adult and I didn't think I was a shallow person."

"Do you have any idea what you were reacting to?"

"I think that it could simply be pride. Pride for Suzanne, for myself, pride for you being married to her. I didn't want anyone to see her that way because if no one saw her, somehow it wouldn't be true. It didn't have to be explained. It was the thing in the middle of that room that we didn't need to talk about."

"But that all changed, didn't it when she could no longer walk," I asked her.

"I can remember when she could only get around on a scooter and then of course, she would not be able to get in and out of the scooter on her own. She would need a wheelchair then."

Caroline's voice choked as she continued. "I knew that she would be confined to one until her last days. At that point, all bets were off. There was no more hiding. The illness had forced itself completely out into the open. And Suzanne guided me through even that, as if I was the one who needed the support."

The following day Caroline sent me this email:

"I had forgotten my reaction to that walker. It was so cumbersome and lumbering. It always reminded me of that Delmore Schwartz Poem, *The Heavy Bear*. In the poem, Schwartz speaks of: "the heavy bear that goes with me." The poem continues:

> That inescapable animal walks with me
> Has followed me since the black womb held,
> Moves where I move, distorting my gesture,
> A caricature, a swollen shadow,

> A stupid clown of the spirit's motive,
> Perplexes and affronts with his own darkness,
> The secret life of belly and bone,
> Opaque, too near, my private, yet unknown,
> Stretches to embrace the very dear
> With whom I would walk without him near,
> Touches her grossly, although a word,
> Would bare my heart and make me clear,
> Stumbles, flounders and strives to be fed
> Dragging me with him in his mouthing care,
> Amid the hundred million of his kind
> The scrimmage of appetite everywhere.

What did people see when they looked at Suzanne? They saw the illness. They saw that heavy bear, not the slim, beautiful, athletic and vibrant woman that my stepmother really was. So often I wanted to scream, No! it's a trick. It's not true. You need to look past the heavy bear to see the truth."

At the end of the week, I reminded the doctor that Suzanne's living will was on file at the nurses' desk. I told him that Suzanne would not wish to be sustained by a machine, if it was certain she would never breathe again on her own. Yet, even as the words bubbled from my lips, I had doubts. We had never discussed the situation at length. Now she had lapsed into a semi-coma and couldn't tell me what she wanted. It was up to me to decide for her. With Caroline at my side, I told the doctor to turn off the respirator.

It didn't happen the way it does in films. There was no last grandstanding, no beatific light suddenly flooding the stark white walls of the hospital room. Instead the gears of bureaucracy ground slowly like a medieval torture instrument. The head of the emergency room deliberated for a few days and then consulted with the ethics committee. The ethics committee considered the matter and gave final approval for the removal of the respirator.

Suzanne was taken off life-support, moved to a private room on the floor below, and given an oxygen mask and low doses of morphine. At the moment the respirator was disconnected, a sensation of disappointment swept through me, as of an event left unfinished. I had expected something momentous, earth-shaking to happen. Was this all there was to it? A human life has been declared over and yet taxis continued humming up and down the avenues. Commuters stopped to pick up dry cleaning, connoitered at newsstands. For them nothing had changed. There was no fanfare, no political action committees, no advocates, not even a family member to object to the termination of her life.

The doctor explained that there was no way to predict when her life would end. During the two days she survived, I spoke to her softly about the things we might have done, the trips we might have taken together. Tibet or Cambodia. Even Alaska. I knew that somewhere down the road I would go to those places alone or with a friend, because they were places Suzanne had always wanted to see. Now I felt obliged to see them for her.

As I talked to her, it struck me that my wife, my companion, my best friend of twenty-eight years would soon be gone, somewhere in the next world if such a place exists. I couldn't imagine the story ending here – the two of us alone in a sterile room with Suzanne gasping for breath and me asking questions that she probably couldn't hear.

"God," I prayed. "Give her back to me just for a second. Just to let her know I'm here. Just let her look at me and smile. Let me know she knows I'm with her." I couldn't bear to think of her feeling alone. I went on talking to her and searching for a sign that she recognized me, that she was aware of my presence standing next to her at the end. The oxygen mask hummed mechanically. The tepid autumn sun leaked through the blinds of the hospital window. Suzanne remained motionless with the faintest flicker of a pulse and nothing more.

    I waited at her bedside, attempting to read the New York Times, but unable to focus. I looked up at Suzanne every few seconds when I heard her making cough-like bursts of sound beneath her oxygen mask. At 6:50 A.M. her breathing changed. The intervals between coughs widened. I reached over the bed and clasped her hands. I knew what was happening, but couldn't bring myself to acknowledge it. I held her hands firmly for ten minutes.

    At seven she stopped breathing. She had died, but her hands remained warm. I took off her oxygen mask and turned my cheek to her mouth and nose. No breath. I put my hand on her heart. No heartbeat. I kissed her softly and whispered, "Thanks for waiting for me." I stayed with her another ten minutes, sharing our final moments together, then walked to the nurse's station to get a doctor to certify her death.

    Snapshots of our life together flooded my mind. A hotel overlooking the Bay of Naples with a cocktail pianist crooning Italian lounge songs. Suzanne and Caroline holding hands, their faces united in solidarity and triumph as they completed the trail in Bryce Canyon. Suzanne emerging from the waters of Bonaire, flinging her arms around me and whispering, "God, your eyes are the color of cobalt blue. I feel they're penetrating me."

When Suzanne died, a burden had been lifted, but the sudden burst of relief didn't last. That day I walked into my apartment for the first time since Suzanne and I had moved into it twenty-four years earlier. The rooms scared me, screaming of departure and absence; the equipment, wheelchairs, electric recliners, an assortment of remote controls now completely useless, irrelevant. Daisy, our cat, followed me wherever I went uttering haunted feral screams that punctuated the icy silence. I turned on more lights, but the apartment seemed dimmer, the furniture and the walls dampened by a gray curtain of emptiness. I wished I'd had a fire place, a burning hearth to huddle in against the rawness of loss and the coming of winter. Suzanne and I had talked every day of our marriage. Who would I talk with now at the end of the day? I looked at her photograph and knew, despite the initial relief, that I had never wanted her out of my life. I had envisioned growing old with her, as I had imagined growing old with my brother, who had died at age sixty-seven of an aneurysm.

When he was young, the physicist Richard P. Feynman married a woman named Arline Greenbaum, whom many described as his soul mate. Arline was diagnosed with tuberculosis shortly before their marriage and given only a few years to live. She died in 1945 at a sanitarium in Albuquerque, where she had moved to be near Richard while he worked on the Manhattan Project in Los Alamos. The tenderness and agony expressed in Feynman's letters demonstrate the ache in his bones to recapture his presence. "I find it hard to understand in my mind what it means to love you after you are dead," he wrote to Arline nearly a year and a half after she had died. "But I still want to comfort and take care of you--and I want you to love me and care for me." Perhaps, he ventured, they could continue to make plans together, but that proved to be impossible, for he had lost his "idea-woman" – the "general instigator of all our wild adventures."

In another letter, Feynman wrote, "You can give me nothing now yet I love you so that you stand in my way of loving anyone else. … But I want you to stand there. You dead, are so much better than anyone else alive."

Fennyman's words reverberate in my head like an echo gathering momentum as I remember the last moments of Suzanne's life, two days after she had been removed from the respirator. In those two days, a bond formed between her dying and my living. The mystery of her image generated a particular kind of love. James Hillman calls this *imaginal love*, an emotion based on a relationship with images.

Harvey A. Kaplan

As I sat in the armchair, the cat cradling into my belly, questions pressed in on me: Why couldn't you wait? Why didn't you give yourself time to process your emotions? Was a week long enough to arrive at an irrevocable decision? Had I done it because I couldn't bear to watch her suffer? Did I honestly feel she would be better off dead? I came back to the same old question. Was it all about me? Had I done it in order to be free – relieved of the burden of constant care and endless anxiety? And now, in this new world, suddenly free from dependency and disease, what would my newfound freedom mean?

I started to read about euthanasia so I could get a bearing on the issues. The arguments for euthanasia or physician-assisted suicide are varied. One goes like this: if the goal of administering morphine to a dying patient is to relieve pain, then the action is based on a different principle than if the goal is to hasten death. Some religions find euthanasia acceptable if the intent is not to cause death, but rather to alleviate pain and suffering. Yet, even within the same religion, opinions are often divided on the issue. Catholicism, however, holds euthanasia or physician-assisted suicide to be an attack on life that no human authority can justify. Catholics maintain that life is a gift from God and all human beings are obliged to respect and protect that gift.

I hoped, were the situation reversed, she would have done the same for me. Yet, when Suzanne and I made out our living wills, we were not near death. And when Suzanne was near death, she was not aware of the documents, not in a position to discuss them, revise them, think through them after several decades. At those moments, so close to the end, when she was unconscious and unable to speak, she was incapable of turning over her decision-making powers to me. How can anyone speak for what might be in another person's mind when the moment of death actually arrives?

Many people have a terror of being trapped on life-support. They conceive of it as a living death. Is it compassionate to spare them that ordeal? Or does acting mercifully and compassionately without clear direction from the dying person, who, being unconscious cannot provide, it, violate the ideal of self-determination? And what about self-determination? If Suzanne had been sufficiently conscious to be asked to decide the question for herself, who would have placed that burden on her? I struggled with all these questions for that long week that Suzanne lay on life-support. Is there a moral distinction between allowing someone to die and actually causing or deliberately hastening that person's death? Some ethicists find no significant distinction between the two. Turning off Suzanne's respirator can be seen as merely standing aside and refusing to block the natural course of events that a fatal disease by then was bound to take. Is that what I did?

Questions such as this elude the simple logic of linear arithmetic. We each have to go through our own configurations of logic to find the answer we can live with. I believe there is a moral distinction between what is called passive and active euthanasia. Passive euthanasia is denying a life-support system; active euthanasia involves taking more aggressive action to end the patient's life. In both cases, compassion may be the motive; yet in both cases, the result is death, and a human being is the agent of terminating life. Although a deliberate termination of a life might still be moral, omission and commission are not the same thing when it comes to euthanasia. In cases of omission, moral agency is always difficult to determine. It is far easier to say who did a thing than to say who did not do it. If what was omitted should have been done, it becomes difficult to determine who is responsible for the omission.

Religious theology teaches that most human actions have mixed outcomes, both good and bad. The most well-intentioned action can have a dire consequence. The use of a narcotic analgesic to manage a terminally ill patient's pain may produce coma or cardiovascular compromise, thus hastening death. While the intention may have been compassionate relief of the patient's suffering, the unintended outcome was death.

Those who advocate for the right to die would say that people have the right to make important decisions about their own lives in pursuit of what they deem to be the good life. This position supports the "mercy killings" administered by Jack Kevorkian. Those who oppose this position cite instances of elderly patients being subtly, and sometimes not so subtly, pressured by family members to end their lives. For them, it is enough to say that killing is wrong because it robs the patient of a continued life and a future invested with plans and dreams that must be respected.

If Suzanne's illness was merciless, her death was merciful. As I have described, about two or three days before the end, she fell into a semi coma. The doctors told me, given her already compromised immune system, there was only a slight chance that her body could stave off the infection she had contracted. Suzanne remained intermittently lucid for another day, while I stayed at her side. I had a feeling she knew I was there, but I am not at all certain. When the oxygen was finally removed, her death was easy, as deaths go, in the sense that the analgesics were floating her out on a tranquil wave. There were no violent teeth of the shark, the bloody frenzy was prevented by opiates and her own rising delirium. A smile of contentment flitted across her lips as she quietly slipped away.

I remember Peggy Lee singing *Is That All There Is?* and I say to myself, so this is what it comes down to; no fanfare, no fancy speeches. She came into my life one evening at a party long ago and now, unfathomably, she glides out of existence. No protests, no political action committees, no advocates, not even a family member to object to the termination of her life.

But during the days following her death questions festered in my mind. Did I consciously think my life with Suzanne would end? Did I feel this was the finish of our relationship? It may sound mystical, but I really didn't think our life together would end. In time I knew the sensation of her presence might fade, that there might be other women in my life, but that didn't mean I would lose her forever. I had a sense that something of her would continue to inhabit my life. The images I had of her and the glow that emanated from those images would hover and guide me, assuring me of the continuity of our relationship.

At the moment the respirator was disconnected an emptiness drained me. The unpleasant disappointment of an event left unfinished. I imagined myself tearing my garments and pounding on my chest and screaming at God in the heavens. "You mean that's all there is to it? A human life has ended and it's over?" Was Suzanne now gone from me forever? Did I just turn and walk away and leave her? It's that how it's done?

No, it's not exactly done that way. You do eventually turn and walk away, but the mourning process begins only when the shock is over. After the numbness is over and the condolence calls stop, memory and desire become active again. We imagine a dead relationship back into life, putting it in perspective. The ghost of the lost person continues to resonate within us. We conjure back their images–the best fragments of memories of our loved one gleam in our remembrance. We breathe life into those images. They fill the recesses of our soul, and the person we loved lives again within us.

When I think back now over the numerous assaults on Suzanne's body, the ankle and wrist fractures she experienced, the two shoulder surgeries, the bi-lateral mastectomy, the countless times she fell in the house and in the streets, not to mention the chronic fatigue and paralysis and cognitive impairment, I still wonder how she endured it all. What gave her courage in the face of such monumental physical destruction? What, if not an indomitable spirit and a soul that refused to submit? Life meant more to her than suffering. She reached out to every relationship she could nurture, everything that brought her closer to nature, to a creative event, to a startling idea. In the final moments of her life, all that had meant life to her was transferred to me. As she died, our souls reunited. I walked out of her room and down the hospital corridor and out into the street, knowing that her soul would continue to live within me.

As I turned toward home, one of my favorite Sinatra songs drifted through my mind. *Moonlight Becomes You.* After the rosary of tears, after the shabby dress of disease is stripped away, the graceful Sinatra lyrics do justice to you. I imagine her. I breathe her into being. Fantasies of her spring before me in the moonlight.

Chapter Twelve

I'll Be Seeing You

Everybody knows about dragons, the enormous, fierce, savage creatures appearing in fairy tales. Mysterious, ferocious beasts that represent the evils fought by human beings. In the world of fantastic animals, the dragon is unique. Many stories portray them as mean and bloodthirsty much like MS, a mysterious, ferocious and destructive illness that must be eradicated.

In one of the great myths regarding dragons, Saint George wanted to show the world that Christians did not have to be meek. The people in the town around Cappadocia tried to calm down the dragon with sacrifices of their best sheep. This worked for awhile, but then the dragon attacked again. The poor people had to give up what they thought would rid the animal of their town, a virgin princess. They sought help and it was George who slay the dragon with the lance he had in his hand while charging with his huge steed. Because of this heroic deed, other Christian Knights sought out to save damsels in distress from dragons, and that is how dragons eventually got slaughtered and became just a myth. My hope is that modern medicine learns a profound lesson from this legend and one day a scientist will come along who will slay the dragons of MS. And yet it doesn't matter. As the tapestry of the world unscrolls new diseases will arise, strange plagues, new viruses, nuclear annihilation. I have learned it would be foolish to think that humans could stop flux.

In *Force of Character*, James Hillman says: "One's remaining image, that unique way of being and doing, left in the minds of others, continues to act upon them–in anecdote, reminiscence, dream, as exemplar, mentoring voice, ancestor–a potent force working in those with lives left to live." After we die, our character endures in the images it ignites in others. To have known Suzanne was to imagine her with all her complex traits, interests, humor, courage, and tenacity. My imagination continues to draw me close to her. And when my imagination brings forth an image of her that is regal, then inspiration blooms.

The images of that person who is no longer on this earth are ours and ours alone. These images are unique. As Harvard Professor of Biology Richard C. Lewontin writes: "Indeed, no two unrelated humans who have ever lived or ever will live are likely to be identical even for the handful of commonest molecular polymorphisms."

Loved ones are preserved in our memories in the stories we tell about them, in the images we hold of them, in the way we recount their histories which allow them to have an even powerful presence in our lives. They exist in our dreams and imagination. We see a photograph of the person in which he or she is young and vital and, much as with a favorite song or piece of music that brings with it a tinge of longing and regret, experience a yearning for them. In a single glance at an old photograph an entire life can glide across the screens of our brain like a movie we once saw and can never forget.

Well-meaning friends sometimes ask me: "Have you gotten over it yet?" I want to reply, "What do you mean by 'it'? If you mean her, I ask you, why should I want to get over her?" I see her face before me and instantly feel wonder at the image. Love does not fade away, it breathes forever within us.

Many of us who have lost a loved one feel a common longing: for one last conversation, one last chance to say that crucial thing, ask that unasked question. Some nights I come home at about 10:30 or 11:00 and sit down in the living room. I pour a glass of chardonnay and look out the window. Scenes of how my life with Suzanne might have been were it not for her illness play out against the darkness. If the gods were to grant me one wish, I would ask to talk to her one last time.

The skyline of New York blazes every night as I ponder certain questions. Buildings flash with electric lights, tourists drift up Broadway, chatting and marveling at the vibrant metropolis. The city reassures me. It never sleeps or dies. It remains a constant circuit of energy. I imagine Suzanne high in the universe, gazing down at the dots of life from a great distance, filled with a great wisdom, finally floating free from her body with wild abandon.

I would tell her that without her I probably would not have understood the true meaning of character. I would say that I recognize something blessed within the constant striving of her soul toward life, toward hope, toward achieving the best of which she was capable. What were our best moments? Our worst? When she heard the original diagnosis did she guess the MS would be as brutal as it turned out to be? The endless blackness of the disability. Her mind at times like a machine that could not spark no matter how much medication tried to ignite it. If she had lived a healthy life, what would her vision would have been for her existence in her sixties and seventies. Did she miss her parents? Could she forgive me for not taking her to Alaska?

The most difficult question I might ask her: What would you have wanted me to do about the respirator? I would assure her that I wanted her to be honest and that I could withstand her honesty. I never heard Suzanne say that she wished she were dead. But her living will stated that she did not wish to be sustained by artificial means. I could never have disconnected the respirator myself, for that would have put me in the direct role of ending her life. But did I have the right to permit her death, even to spare her from suffering?

Our unique characteristics are perpetuated when they are viewed as images. The individuality of the person becomes a shifting kaleidoscope, each of us becoming more unique, instable and complex. If we all are a conglomeration of complex images then to know a person we must first imagine and absorb his or her various images. To remain close to someone, whether that person is still living or not, we must connect with that person through the imagination. If our love is to survive, it needs to imagine, otherwise it falls into sentiment and boredom. If we view life this way then relationships fail not because we have stopped loving but because we first stopped imagining.

I received a postcard from an old friend of Suzanne's who lives in Germany half the year and in Capetown the other half. I called her to tell her of Suzanne's death, but couldn't get through, so then I wrote, but the letter was not delivered. Now I picked up the phone again, and this time Gisela answered from Stuttgart.

"Harvey," she asked. "What is the reason you are calling me? Something has happened to Suzanne?"

I opened my mouth to tell her, but the words froze in my throat. I choked with despair, yet I tried again.

At once Gisela realized what I was trying to say. "When did this happen?"

"Eight months ago."

"Poor Suzanne," the sound of a hushed sobbing emerged from the black maw of the receiver. "Was she in much pain? Please tell me."

I reassured her that Suzanne died comfortably with an oxygen mask and a morphine drip. Her face was peaceful. Gisela prompted me for details. I told her about the hospital, the infection, the respirator.

"Every opera I go to, I will feel Suzanne sitting along side me. I think when we hang up I am going to go to pieces. I can feel it in my heart already." She asked me to come to Europe soon so we could talk more.

I understand what Gisela meant when she tells me that she can't listen to opera without feeling Suzanne's presence. When I enjoy an experience I know Suzanne loved, I feel her with me. As I look out the window of the condo on a rainy day and see the glistening beads of the rain pounding down across the iridescent surface of the lake, I remember how Suzanne loved to watch the rain hitting the water. Where does my love – meant only for her – go now? Who receives it? Even as I ask these questions, I know that she is still my love, not entirely in sadness, yet not fully in joy.

Ten months after Suzanne's death, it was August – the traditional month for psychotherapists to take their vacations. For the first time in twenty-eight years, I thought about planning a vacation without Suzanne. A friend of mine mentioned a small psychoanalytic conference in South Africa. After the conference, about fifteen people would tour the country and visit animal preserves. I knew most of the people from various analytic societies. At least I won't be alone, I thought making the reservation. The agent announced there would be an extra charge for my new status in life, a "single supplement."

I found the colleagues on the South Africa trip easy to get along with. The history of South Africa was grim, but fascinating. On a damp oppressive afternoon, the bus dropped us off at the Capetown Botanical Gardens. A gentle rain misted the air, producing an atmospheric dampness that adhered to every surface of my skin. I thought of the last time I had visited gardens similar to these. Five years earlier, Suzanne and I had taken a trip with Gisela to the New York Botanical Gardens. Images of that afternoon spread through me, filling me with a greater emptiness.

The three of us, Suzanne on her scooter, proceeded leisurely through the lush gardens nestled in the East Bronx adjacent to Fordham University. We spent about an hour walking along the garden paths until we came to a large greenhouse that was home to rare orchids and bougainvillea. As we moved through the greenhouse, I found myself walking alone, Suzanne and Gisela having dropped back behind me, stopping to admire particular plants. Soon the murmur of their voices was lost in the thick humidified air. I left the greenhouse and sat on a bench just outside to wait for them. After about forty-five minutes, my impatience bubbled up. I went back inside to see what was keeping them. I found them amid the flowering plants deep in conversation.

"Do you have any idea how long you've been talking?" I snapped.

"No." Suzanne's voice was defiant. "We don't know and we don't care. We've been catching each other up on our lives."

"Come on Harvey," Gisela chimed in. "I don't see her that often, these moments are precious to us."

"That's wonderful for you two," I said. "But I'm the one who's waiting." They both burst out laughing.

"Your impatience again." Suzanne smiled and insisted that I give them another half hour. I went outside and sat down on my bench again, feeling annoyed, but impressed by how attuned they were to one another and happy that Suzanne had such a close friend.

On that oppressive August day in South Africa, as I walked through the Capetown Botanical Gardens alone, a woman from the tour approached me.

"Someone told me that you lost your wife not too long ago," she greeted me "I want to tell you how sorry I am."

I smiled and thanked her.

"I lost my husband a few years earlier," she offered. "I was in this boat yesterday, and as it left the harbor and started out to sea, I suddenly burst into tears. I thought how he would have loved this. His loss still lays so heavily on my mind."

I explained that I hadn't thought I would mind taking this vacation on my own until I saw these gardens and realized how much Suzanne would have loved them. As I said it, I felt how easily the tears welled up in my eyes. I couldn't go on talking. Her eyes glowed with compassion and then she walked away from me, not wanting to interfere with my grief. As I strolled through the gardens, I could almost hear Suzanne's voice whispering about the intoxicating fragrance of the flowers and how glad she was that I walked slowly, observing the foliage, not rushing through them.

Back in New York a few weeks later that woman called me. She wanted to get together for drinks. We met at a bar on 57th Street and talked of loss, the trip across continents, the differences between friendship and romantic love, the adjustment to traveling as a single supplement and feeling marginalized.

At the Capetown pool, two kids cavorted in the green trees laughing and speaking in German. I let the language resonate within me and went on reading. Suzanne was fluent in German. The years she spent there, the lover she had whom she never spoke of, were an exotic mystery in my unconscious. I put down the book and listened to the chatter of the boys. I couldn't understand a word of what they were saying, but it was obvious that they were happy and playful. Death was a far away illusion, a concept existing in fairy tales, where the dead were awakened with a kiss.

For Suzanne, the symphony of life was never finished. There was no third movement, no third act. We never had the pleasure of growing old together. She never rose to the apex of her intended profession. She never cradled our children to her breast or agonized with them over college application essays. I lounged by the pool in South Africa, growing old alone for both of us.

The isolation of a strange country and the forced mirth of a disappointing trip pulled at me. The vacation was a rich dessert but my appetite had abandoned me. I lounged by the pool in South Africa, growing old alone, for both of us.

While in Capetown, I often had a drink at the hotel bar with Helen, another "single supplement" on the trip. Helen had known Suzanne from the Freudian Society. She asked me about Kenya where similar conditions concerning the Land Rover and the ride to the animal preserves had prevailed. I told her I was younger then and there were two of us, but the conditions in Kenya were worse because the vehicle was smaller and had more people jammed into it. She asked me how Suzanne felt about it. I told her it was hard to remember, but Suzanne rarely complained about anything and she loved the flowers at the Royal Kenyan Hotel. Helen nodded and said that in all the years she had known Suzanne she never heard her complain about anything.

When I taxied back from the airport, I wondered why, after ten months, the apartment still felt so empty. But why shouldn't it, I ask myself, when the person I loved and talked with every day for twenty-eight years is gone? I sat in the stillness of the night, not yet ready for newspapers or television, waiting to clear my mind.

Over the next few days, uneasy dreams washed over me, images of hospitals and gardens and vast African plains where gazelles were brought down in the bloody jaws of a lioness. Throughout the fall I kept thinking of the prison where the Apartheid regime had confined Nelson Mandela. His cell was no more than 12 by 14 feet. How could he have endured it all those years? What strength of character and mind he had to have to tolerate the isolation and the hatred and then after decades to have come out of prison without bitterness for his oppressors. Yet Mandela had the capacity to forgive. His forgiveness united his country and prevented centuries of continued bloodshed and inhumanity. Certainly, he was one of the great heroes of all time. Through the entire fall the thought of Mandela stayed with me.

In the Jewish faith, it is customary to have an unveiling within the first year of a loved one's death. This involves buying a headstone and engraving it with the name of the deceased, date of birth, date of death, and an epitaph. When I received the letter from the cemetery telling me that Suzanne's headstone was in place, I planned an unveiling ceremony with family and a few friends. I decided not to wait a full year before having the unveiling. I scheduled it for noon on Sunday, September 25. September had been mild, and I didn't want to risk waiting for the November chill. Unveilings have psychological significance and I was depressed by the implication of this ceremony. The year of mourning had ended, and it was time to let her go and get on with life.

I wanted a small group around me, and this would include my daughter, my sister-in-law, my niece and her child, and my nephew and his wife. I also wanted Marty and Gail two friends who had been an integral part of our social life both in Montague, New Jersey, and in New York.

We drove the fifteen miles to the cemetery in New Jersey, where my brother, mother, and father are also buried. I knew I would visit each of their graves later that day. It took a few moments to locate Suzanne's grave. When I came upon it, I had a strange feeling that the headstone was a substitute for Suzanne. My wife has gone forever, I thought, and what is left of her is an engraved slab of gray stone.

Harvey A. Kaplan

SUZANNE B. KAPLAN
SO DEARLY LOVED
CHERISHED FOREVER
DECEMBER 4, 1941 - NOVEMBER 2, 2004

For a moment, I imagined her body lying beneath the soil, still and peaceful. As I conjured up the image of her face, I still could not separate the wounded, disabled look from the look of health and radiance she bore when we first met. The images were a slow continuous blur.

As we assembled around her grave, I wondered how Suzanne had managed to integrate all the many changes that took place in her body and mind, the movement from health to disability, from energy to dependency, from a way of seeing the world as a great adventure to a place that was filled with obstacles and had to be negotiated with care.

I stood before the eight people at the gravesite and spoke the words I had prepared. Words I had run through my mind many times, hoping familiarity with my text would keep me from breaking down while actually delivering it. It didn't. As I talked about Suzanne's innate goodness and beauty, I couldn't restrain my tear as I continued with my speech, explaining that to the outside world our relationship may have appeared to be a burden on me, but that in fact her illness had enhanced my life. It brought us closer together and made me a better man. Not a day went by that I didn't call her three or four times to ask what was going on at home and how she was feeling. Not a day went by that I didn't wonder what I could do to make things easier for her. What could I buy for her or have built or constructed for her? By the time I got home in the evenings, it seemed we had never been apart. I told my family and friends how much Suzanne meant to me and how she became a catalyst in my life, spurring me on to accomplish things I had never thought possible. I told them how her support, motivation, and faith in me over the years substantiated a part of me I thought was lacking. I told them how my love for her gave meaning to my life.

I told stories to illustrate different aspects of Suzanne's character and to show how sensitively she responded not only to me, but to all her friends. I spoke of how people came to love her and to admire the sincerity and courage with which she led her life. I told my favorite story of her unstinting support for my hugely misconceived plan to take piano lessons late in life, and of how, when I finally came to my senses about this and wanted to give the piano to my ex-wife, she supported that plan as well. I ended with another favorite story, the one about the present Suzanne gave me on my fiftieth – that fantastic photograph of Frank Sinatra, signed: "To Harvey, Happy Birthday. Frank Sinatra."

I closed with a prayer, and it was over. I knew I would come out here soon again and spend more time with her, quietly and alone. The event had been too rushed for me, crowded with formal ritual and my own block of not wanting to display my naked feelings. What I needed was time to linger and talk to her in my own fashion. I would do that soon.

We then moved on to my brother Don's grave. From there I went to my parents' site. It was over for that day, and I felt I had orchestrated it well.

We drove back to the city, where I opened my apartment to a group of about twenty-five people. We celebrated Suzanne's life with joy, which I knew was what she would have wanted. "Put the mourning behind you," I could hear her low throaty whispering. "Remember me with happiness."

I listen to "I've Got You Under My Skin," and I get stuck on her all over again. The ghost of past love emerges from a shimmering bronzed leaf falling from a tree as summer ends and the cycle of fall begins. Soon the trees will become skeletal. Sinking down into the armchair, I remember her vivacious brown eyes and the lively lilt in her voice at the long-ago party saying, "There is no time like the present."

References

Breslow, Rachelle. *Who Said So?* Berkeley: Celestial Publishing. 1991.

Broyard, Anatole. *Intoxicated by My Illness: And Other Writings on Life andDeath,* Com. And ed. Alexandra Broyard (New York: Clarkson N. Potter, 1992.

Feigelson, Carolyn. "Personality Death, Object Loss, and the Uncanny," *Int. J. Psycho-Anal.*, 1993, vol. 74, pp.331-345.

Fisher, Helen. *Anatomy of Love.* New York: Random House Publishing Group. 1992.

Frank, Arthur W. *At the Will of the Body.* Boston: Houghton Mifflin Co. 1991.

Frank, Arthur W. *The Wounded Storyteller.* Chicago: The University of Chicago Press. 1995.

Garr, Teri. *Speedbumps.* New York: Hudson Street Press, 2005.

Hillman, James. *The Soul's Code, In Search of Character and Calling.* New York: Warner Books Edition, 1996.

_____*The Force of Character and the Lasting Life.* New York: Random House, 1999.

_____*Healing Fiction.* Barrytown: Open Studio, Ltd., 1983.

Leavy, S.A. "John Keats's Psychology of Creative Imagination, *Psychoanal.Q.,* 1970, vol.39, pp. 173-197.

MacFarline, Ellen Burstein. *Legwork.* New York: Charles Scribner's Sons. 1994.

Mairs, Nancy. *Voice Lessons: On Becoming a (Woman) Writer.* Boston: Beacon Press, 1994.

Manning, Michael. *Euthanasia and Physician-Assisted Suicide. Killing or Caring.* New York: Paulist Press. 1998.

Munker, Dona. "Enchantment and Biographical Passion," *American Imago,* 1997, vol. 54, pp.377-397.

Murphy, Robert F. *The Body Silent.* New York: Henry Holt and Co. 1987.

Novak, Michael. *The Joy of Sports.* Lanham: Madison Books, 1994.

Radner, Gilda. *It's Always Something.* New York: Avon Books, 1989

Schank, Roger C. *Tell me a Story: A New Look at Real and Artificial Memory.* New York: Scribners, 1990.

Schafer, Roy. *The Analytic Attitude.* New York: Basic Books Inc., 1983.

Schwartz, Delmore. *Selected Poems.* New York: New Directions., 1967

Sternberg, Robert J. *Love is a Story: A New Theory of Relationships.* Oxford University Press. 1998.

Sternberg, Robert J. & Barnes, Michael, J. Editors. *The Psychology of Love.* New Haven: Yale University Press. 1988.

Webster, Barbara D. *All of a Piece: A Life with Multiple Sclerosis.* Baltimore: The Johns Hopkins University Press. 1989.

Wineapple, Brenda. "Mourning Becomes Biography," *American Imago,* 1997, vol. 54, pp. 437-451.

Young-Bruehl, Elisabeth & Bethelard, Faith. *Cherishment: A Psychology of the Heart.* New York: The Free Press, 2000.

Annotated References

Breslow, Rachelle. *Who Said So?* Berkeley: Celestial Publishing. 1991.
This is a powerful and very personal story of Rachelle's struggle towards health and healing, filled with the valuable lessons she learned along the way. It shows how our thoughts and beliefs can have a strong affect on our immune system. She takes an impressive stand to try and heal and regain her health with positive thinking.

Broyard, Anatole. *Intoxicated by My Illness: And Other Writings on Life and Death,* Com. And ed. Alexandra Broyard (New York: Clarkson N. Potter, 1992.
This is a delightful book and while it is charming and at times moving, it maintains a consistently high level of understanding and wisdom about feeling ill and with the many personal changes that go along with it.

Feigelson, Carolyn. "Personality Death, Object Loss, and the Uncanny," *Int. J. Psycho-Anal.*, 1993, vol. 74, pp.331-345.
This article highlights the conflict of coming to grips with loving a spouse who has changed their character and appearance because of an injury. Dr. Feigelson grappled with finding a way to come to terms with her husband's head injury and she highlights the many issues that ensue in this process. He looks differently to her and acts in odd ways. She realizes that this not the person she originally married and now she needs to come to grips with this and find how to love this person with all the changes he has undergone.

Fisher, Helen. *Anatomy of Love.* **New York: Random House Publishing Group. 1992.**
Dr. Fisher explains the concept of love maps which is one of the ways psychology tries to account for the mysteries of being seized by love. Particular characteristics of past experiences form a schema that you fall for when a person crosses your path who seems to have the attributes of your love map. It's as if you have been waiting to meet this person all your life. When your spouse becomes disabled you must remember what you originally found so beguiling in them. This continues your love for them.

Frank, Arthur W. *At the Will of the Body.* **Boston: Houghton Mifflin Co. 1991.**
In this book, Dr. Frank presents a unique account of serious illness. Courage, fear, denial, anger, hope- nothing is left out as he takes us on a guided tour of his experience with close-to-the-bone honesty. He shows us the importance of facing the illness not pushing it away from ourselves. It's a tough account of a serious illness.

Frank, Arthur W. *The Wounded Storyteller.* **Chicago: The University of Chicago Press. 1995.**
Dr. Frank presents us with the many different ways of constructing a story of a sickness. His unique contribution is elucidating three basic narratives that attempt to come to grips with illness. He calls them the *Restitution Narrative, Chaos Narrative and Quest Narrative.* This is an important contribution because it shows us how we come to understand our experience as we go through coping with illness. And it highlights the way we are go about developing our own personal narrative of our illness.

Garr, Teri. *Speedbumps.* **New York: Hudson Street Press, 2005.**
By the time she was thirty, Teri had become known as one of Hollywood's best-loved comic actresses. And then in October 2002, she announced on national television that she had multiple sclerosis. Since then she has become a leading advocate in raising awareness for

MS traveling around the country speaking to corporations, physicians, and patients about her experience. Within these pages you come to know a person who is so highly invested in helping others and finding a cure. She evolves as a true role model of someone who both faces their illness head on and then goes out and educates the public about the importance of funding and advancing a cure for multiple sclerosis.

Hillman, James. *The Soul's Code, In Search of Character and Calling.* **New York: Warner Books Edition, 1996.**
_____*The Force of Character and the Lasting Life.* **New York: Random House, 1999.**
_____*Healing Fiction.* **Barrytown: Open Studio, Ltd., 1983.**
In these books, Hillman presents a vital new approach in understanding our character and soul. He restores a passion, uniqueness, destiny and childhood to every human life. It enabled me to find a deeper kind of love for my wife and search for avenues of appreciation both for what she was going through and for her courage in facing this difficult disease. Locating the soul of the loved one is a complicated undertaking but one that leads to a different kind of compassion for our love of the other.

Leavy, S.A. "John Keats's Psychology of Creative Imagination, *Psychoanal.Q.,* **1970, vol.39, pp. 173-197.**
It was Keats who talked of the vale of soul making. This article highlights the genius of Keats and his ability to find purpose and importance in creating a life that matters.

MacFarline, Ellen Burstein. *Legwork.* **New York: Charles Scribner's Sons. 1994.**
This is a sad story of how she was cheated by believing in a doctor who professed to curing multiple sclerosis. Torn between dwelling on this devastating experience and putting it behind her, she opted to go after the doctor to make sure that he did not hurt any one else. Her resilience and strength leaps out of these pages and we come away

with realizing the importance of having a conviction about what action we need to take to right a wrong.

Mairs, Nancy. *Ordinary Time*. Boston: Beacon Press, 1994.
This is a seemingly casual, often humorous tale of a woman's struggle to find out who she is and, if there a God, what she may be asking. It is filled a kind of friendly, compassionate wisdom. Her stories abound with wit and above all, wisdom.

Manning, Michael. *Euthanasia and Physician-Assisted Suicide. Killing or Caring.*New York: Paulist Press. 1998.
This is a very informative book that describes the historical background and conceptual framework within which the current debate over euthanasia and physician-assisted suicide is taking place. He explores the argument from both a philosophical and medical consideration. Lastly, he explains the arguments for and against euthanasia and physician-assisted suicide in a clear and evenhanded manner.

Munker, Dona. "Enchantment and Biographical Passion," *American Imago*, 1997, vol. 54, pp.377-397.
Here, Dr. Munker explores the relationship that develops between the writer and the person that is being written about. There needs to be a kind of enchantment toward the subject matter as if to affirm the uniqueness of this person and how she or he has impacted the writer's life. In some ways, we can almost come to love the person whose pages we are constructing.

Murphy, Robert F. *The Body Silent*. New York: Henry Holt and Co. 1987.
This is a deeply personal narrative that comes to grips with the psychological and social effects of a tumor of the spinal cord that began as barely noticeable muscle spasms and within a decade had developed into a still-deepening quadriplegia. This is a story about life and the living and the triumph of mind and spirit over atrophy of the body. He sees disability as an assault upon a person's identity and a

disruption of his ties with others. He started writing the book when he was told of the awful consequences that the tumor would follow. He doesn't look back as he writes it in the present.

Novak, Michael. *The Joy of Sports.* **Lanham: Madison Books, 1994.**
Novak finds a great deal of passion in sports, and writes with an excitement and exhilaration about how sports fill us with idealized versions of life. I thought about how a similar excitement could be generated when we look at how the disabled cope with their illness. As if this was the real life metaphor for explaining courage, fortitude and the ability not to give up in the face of overwhelming odds. They are the true heroes because they are on the battlefield day in and day out.

Radner, Gilda. *It's Always Something.* **New York: Avon Books, 1989**
Radner writes with the kind of humor that touches our souls. This is so real, so meaningful of how she coped with her cancer. In her journey with illness, she shows us what it means to find a deeper meaning in the challenge to stay alive.

Schank, Roger C. *Tell me a Story: A New Look at Real and Artificial Memory.* **New York: Scribners, 1990.**
I found this book helpful in that Schank shows how the stories we tell relate to our memories we have of our experience. Telling stories and listening to other people's stories shape the memories we have of our experience. This relates closely to the disabled because they need to tell their stories in a way that helps and guides them through the perils of their disease.

Schafer, Roy. *The Analytic Attitude.* **New York: Basic Books Inc., 1983.**
As a psychotherapist, I found similarities between the analytic process and caring for a disabled partner. Schafer stress the need to establish an "atmosphere of safety" in relation to the dangers of personal change. His

main focus is on the narrative features that each of us develop over time and he shows how they are used to develop an account of the past and the present that helps to construct a coherent life history.

Schwartz, Delmore. *Selected Poems.* **New York: New Directions., 1967.**
Schwartz's poetry can often be used to describe any malady. He is able to touch the sensitive strains of illness in its multiforms.

Sternberg, Robert J. *Love is a Story: A New Theory of Relationships.* **Oxford University Press. 1998.**
Sternberg, Robert J. & Barnes, Michael, J. Editors. *The Psychology of Love.* **New Haven: Yale University Press. 1988.**
Sternberg two books deals with the idea of what factors go into falling in love. Why do some relationships work so smoothly and others go haywire. He talks about unconscious perceptions that guide our romantic choices. In the case of having a disability enter the relationship, I found Sternberg very helpful in that we can revise our love stories and develop new roles and new kinds of love stories.

Webster, Barbara D. *All of a Piece: A Life with Multiple Sclerosis.* **Baltimore: The Johns Hopkins University Press. 1989.**
In this book, Webster captures a sense of loss she has about what the MS will do to her in the future. It took fourteen years for her to find the correct diagnosis and she couldn't understand the draining fatigue, or the weakness and stumbling gait. She writes about her growing awareness of the emotional and psychological consequences that the disease took and how it affected her self-esteem. Her story is so poignant and insightful and I think anyone with a disability will find parts of themselves in her story.

Wineapple, Brenda. "Mourning Becomes Biography," *American Imago,* **1997, vol. 54, pp. 437-451.**
An interesting aspect of writing a memoir or a biography is how it helps us mourn the person we are writing about. The process of

mourning which we all go through when a loved one dies can be negotiated through the writing of a biography about them. In this writing we are able to mourn them and at the same time let them go.

Young-Bruehl, Elisabeth & Bethelard, Faith. *Cherishment: A Psychology of the Heart.* **New York: The Free Press, 2000.**
The authors provide a wholly original way of thinking about familiar concepts such as love, attachment and care, showing how deep-seated disappointments and fears of dependency can disrupt a relationship when disability enters the picture. Cherishment has much to do with attuning sensitively to the ways people express their need for affection in the details of daily life and relationships. More importantly we come to realize the need to construct a safe environment for the disabled, one that would maximize their personal growth.

www.ingramcontent.com/pod-product-compliance
Lightning Source LLC
Chambersburg PA
CBHW070609300426
44113CB00010B/1470